NEW TESTAMENT MESSAGE

A Biblical-Theological Commentary

Wilfrid Harrington, O.P. and Donald Senior, C.P.
EDITORS

New Testament Message, Volume 7

THE PARABLES

Madeleine I. Boucher

Michael Glazier, Inc.
Wilmington, Delaware

MICHAEL GLAZIER, INC.
1210 King Street
Wilmington, Delaware 19801

Library of Congress Catalog Card Number: 80-85421
International Standard Book Number: 0-89453-130-1
New Testament Message series: 0-89453-123-9

Printed in the United States of America by Abbey Press

CONTENTS

EDITORS' PREFACE

New Testament Message is a commentary series designed to bring the best of biblical scholarship to a wide audience. Anyone who is sensitive to the mood of the church today is aware of a deep craving for the Word of God. This interest in reading and praying the scriptures is not confined to a religious elite. The desire to strengthen one's faith and to mature in prayer has brought Christians of all types and all ages to discover the beauty of the biblical message. Our age has also been heir to an avalanche of biblical scholarship. Recent archaeological finds, new manuscript evidence, and the increasing volume of specialized studies on the Bible have made possible a much more profound penetration of the biblical message. But the flood of information and its technical nature keeps much of this scholarship out of the hands of the Christian who is eager to learn but is not a specialist. *New Testament Message* is a response to this need.

The subtitle of the series is significant: "A Biblical-Theological Commentary." Each volume in the series, while drawing on up-to-date scholarship, concentrates on bringing to the fore in understandable terms the specific message of each biblical author. The essay-format (rather than a word-by-word commentary) helps the reader savor the beauty and power of the biblical message and, at the same time, understand the sensitive task of responsible biblical interpretation.

A distinctive feature of the series is the amount of space given to the "neglected" New Testament writings, such as Colossians, James, Jude, the Pastoral Letters, the Letters of Peter and John. These briefer biblical books make a significant but often overlooked contribution to the richness of the New Testament. By assigning larger than normal coverage to these books, the series hopes to give these parts of Scripture the attention they deserve.

Because *New Testament Message* is aimed at the entire English speaking world, it is a collaborative effort of international proportions. The twenty-two contributors represent biblical scholarship in North America, Britain, Ireland and Australia. Each of the contributors is a recognized expert in his or her field, has published widely, and has been chosen because of a proven ability to communicate at a popular level. And, while all of the contributors are Roman Catholic, their work is addressed to the Christian community as a whole. The New Testament is the patrimony of all Christians.It is the hope of all concerned with this series that it will bring a fuller appreciation of God's saving Word to his people.

Wilfrid Harrington, O.P.
Donald Senior, C.P.

INTRODUCTION

THE IMPORTANCE of the parables can hardly be overestimated. They comprise a substantial part of the recorded preaching of Jesus. The parables are generally regarded by scholars as among the sayings which we can confidently ascribe to the historical Jesus; they are, for the most part, authentic words of Jesus. Moreover, all of the great themes of Jesus' preaching are struck in the parables. Perhaps no part of the Gospels, then, can better put us into touch with the mind of Jesus Christ than the parables. They still today present us with the challenge with which Jesus encountered his hearers in first-century Palestine. These little stories (together with the Lord's Prayer and the Beatitudes) are the best known of all Jesus' words. It is a measure of the value which the Church places upon them that every parable without exception occurs in the Sunday lectionary readings.

This book is divided into two parts. Part I looks at the parable as a literary artifact. In these chapters, I have attempted to make clear what a parable is (its structure) and how it is intended to function (its purpose). This part of the book will, I hope, help to show why the parable has been such an extraordinarily effective preaching device in the ministry of Jesus and in the life of the Church.

Part II provides a brief commentary on each parable (its meaning). In these chapters I have attempted to elucidate what Jesus says by means of these stories. It will be noted that all of the parables are from the Synoptic Gospels, that is, the Gospels of Mark, Matthew, and Luke. That is quite simply because there are no parables in the Gospel of John; there Jesus employs a different method of preaching. (The only passage which could conceivably be included is the Good Shepherd in Jn 10:1–18; but in my judgment that is not a true parable.)

This book has been written, then, with the aim of explaining the structure, purpose, and meaning of the parables of Jesus.

Part One What is a Parable?

1. INTRODUCING THE PARABLES

A. The Parable in the Ancient World

WHEN JESUS PREACHED so strikingly in parables, he did not create a new literary genre. Rather, he made brilliant use of a genre which was already of long tradition and which was familiar to all throughout the Mediterranean world. In Greece and Rome, parables were employed by rhetoricians, politicians and philosophers. Perhaps the most illustrious among those who made use of them were Socrates and Aristotle. An interesting question is to what extent the classical parables are like those of the Bible. (The reader may wish to peruse Aristotle's discussion of the parable in *The "Art" of Rhetoric*, Book II.) In Israel, parables were uttered by prophets and wise women and men. They appear even in the oldest books of the Old Testament. Parables were often used by Jewish rabbis who were contemporaries of Jesus.

A famous and quite ancient Old Testament example is the parable of the Ewe Lamb which the prophet Nathan addressed to David. After the king had arranged the death of Bathsheba's husband on the battlefield so that he might himself marry Bathsheba, Nathan told him this story:

> **12** There were two men in a certain city, the one rich and the other poor. [2]The rich man had very many flocks and herds; [3]but the poor man had nothing but one little ewe lamb, which he had bought. And he brought it up, and it

> grew up with him and with his children; it used to eat of his morsel, and drink from his cup, and lie in his bosom, and it was like a daughter to him. [4]Now there came a traveler to the rich man, and he was unwilling to take one of his own flock or herd to prepare for the wayfarer who had come to him, but he took the poor man's lamb, and prepared it for the man who had come to him.
>
> (2 Sam 12:1-4)

When David condemned the man who had done this as deserving to die, Nathan revealed that the story was a parable, saying, "You are the man" (v. 7). For other Old Testament parables see 2 Sam 14:5-13; 1 Kgs 20:39-42; Isa 5:1-7; 28:23-29; Ezek 17:1-24; 19:1-14; 20:45-49; 24:3-14.

The rabbinic parables are of course the closest in both time and place to those of Jesus. The following example is interesting for its similarity to the Gospel parable of the Two Builders (Mt 7:24-27; Lk 6:47-49):

> He whose wisdom exceeds his works, to what may he be likened? To a tree whose branches are numerous but whose roots are few. The wind comes along and uproots it and sweeps it down.... But he whose works exceed his wisdom, to what may he be likened? To a tree whose branches are few but whose roots are numerous. Then even if all the winds of the world come along and blow against it they cannot stir it from its place....
>
> (*Pirqe Aboth* III. 18)

The parables which most closely resemble Jesus' are those in the Old Testament and rabbinic literature. These Semitic parables (as distinct from the classical) are no doubt the predecessors of those we find preserved in the Synoptic Gospels.

Anyone who compares the parables in the Gospels with those in other sources is led to conclude that Jesus was a master of the genre, perhaps its most brilliant author ever. Even today parables, and in particular those of Jesus, remain among the most beautiful and memorable works in the history of literature.

B. The Term "Parable"

It is well to distinguish at the outset between the *term* "parable" and the *literary class*, and to describe both as clearly as possible. In the ancient sources the term and the literary compositions do not neatly and exactly coincide, as we might wish they would. Therefore distinguishing between the term and the class helps to ensure clarity in our discussion of the subject.

We begin with the term. The word "parable"—*mashal* in Hebrew, *parabolē* in Greek—had a wide range of meanings in both the Bible and the classical literature. Today, however, we do not employ the word in all of those ways. The term "parable" is not, and indeed *should not* be, used in the same senses in scholarly discussion today as it was in antiquity. The only meaning which we generally attach to it today is the fifth and last meaning given below. This restriction is not in itself a problem. It means only that we deliberately use the term more precisely and rigorously than did the ancients, as we should.

Following are examples of the various uses of *"parabolē"* in the New Testament. (1) In the Gospels the word can mean "proverb," as when it refers to the saying, "Physician, heal yourself" (Lk 4:23). (2) It can also refer to the kind of speech called "wisdom saying," which usually consists of two or three parallel lines. The following wisdom saying (called *parabolē*) teaches, by roundabout speech, that it is not the food which goes into the body (the cultic-ritual), but the thoughts, words and deeds which come out of the heart (the ethical) that matter before God:

> There is nothing outside a man which by going into him
> can defile him;
> but the things which come out of a man are what defile him.
> (Mk 7:15; cf. Mt 15:11)

(3) The term *parabolē* is sometimes employed of a slightly developed comparison, as in this lesson drawn from the fig tree: "as soon as its branch becomes tender and puts forth

its leaves, you know that summer is near"; so when certain things happen the disciples will know that the coming of the Son of man is at hand (Mk 13:28-29; cf. Mt 24:32-33; Lk 21:29-31). (4) In the only two New Testament occurrences outside the Gospels, *parabolē* means "symbol" and "figurative speech" (Heb 9:9; 11:19). (5) Finally, the word *parabolē* refers to the Gospel stories which we today commonly call "parables," the more or less extended stories such as the Sower, the Mustard Seed, the Lost Sheep, the Great Feast.

Thus the term, in antiquity, had no precise or fixed definition. It could refer to a wide variety of speeches. The meaning it carried for the ancients was that of any language that was somehow striking or out of the ordinary. It was used of speech that included similes and metaphors, circumlocution (as in the wisdom saying above), and many other devices employed to ornament speech. Often, but not always, the *parabolē* was an implied comparison (as between the coming of the Son of man and the budding fig tree). It should be added that in the Bible there was a tradition of understanding the *parabolē* as mysterious speech, a view which had to do with the aspect of comparison; this understanding will be discussed below.

Since the words *mashal* and *parabolē* were undefined and in flux in antiquity, then it is best for us consciously to adopt a more scientific definition, and to restrict the term "parable" to the fifth meaning given above; this is the literary class described in the following section. For the other kinds of speech mentioned above, it is best to use terms such as those employed there—for example, "proverb" and "wisdom saying."

C. The Literary Class

We wish, then, to define the term "parable" sharply, to have an accurate and precise meaning of the word, and to use it consistently to refer to one particular kind of literature. In modern usage the word should be, and usually is, reserved for those stories which are drawn from ordinary, everyday life, which convey a religious or moral lesson, quite indirectly, and which are intended to convince or persuade, to bring the hearer to decision or action. Examples from the Gospels are the Leaven (Mt 13:33; Lk 13:20-21), the Good Samaritan (Lk 10:29-37) and the Prodigal Son (Lk 15:11-32). It would be well at this point to isolate the four elements in the concise description just given, and to explain them somewhat more fully.

(1) Every parable is a *narrative*, that is, every parable tells a story. The parables belong to popular story-telling or folk literature. Some of these stories are very concise (e.g. the Treasure, Mt 13:44), others are more developed (e.g. the Prodigal Son, Lk 15:11-32). These little narratives are taken from real life, from nature or the human scene. They are simple and realistic stories, drawn from the everyday life of the household, the kitchen, farming and fishing, the courtroom, temple worship. With these marvelous little stories Jesus could express his teaching in a vivid and memorable way.

(2) The parables are stories, but they are also much more. They are not merely tales about the growth of a mustard seed, a catch of fish, a widow who won't take no for an answer. They are intended to convey a lesson. If they were not, they would really have no point at all. The parables have two levels of meaning: the story itself, which is the literal meaning; and the point or lesson, popularly called the figurative meaning but more accurately called the *tropical* meaning (pronounced *trope-ical*). The point or lesson is conveyed indirectly, often only implicitly. For example, the Mustard Seed (Mk 4:30-32; Mt 13:31-32; Lk 13:18-19) teaches a lesson about the reign of God, its small, humble beginnings in the ministry of Jesus and its final, full splendor at the end-time. The lesson of the Fishnet (Mt 13:47-50) is that we must patiently allow the good and the bad to coexist in the world until the final judgement, when God himself will separate them. The point of the Persistent Widow (Lk 18:1-8) is that God will certainly bring

deliverance to his elect. Again, the story we are told (the Mustard Seed, the Fishnet, the Persistent Widow) is the literal meaning; its point or lesson is the tropical meaning (which we usually but somewhat inaccurately call figurative meaning). Thus every parable has two levels of meaning.

(3) The purpose of the parables is not merely to entertain, as may be the case with other folk stories. Their purpose is far more important. It is to bring about a change of mind, or better a change of heart, in the hearer, perhaps to move the hearer to conversion. One of the most important points to understand about the parables is that they present a challenge. Their message is indeed radical, and is not easily ignored. The hearer of a parable can hardly remain neutral, but must accept or reject its point, must act or fail to act on the lesson. This being their purpose, the parables are *rhetorical*; they belong to the broad class of literature called rhetoric, literature which has as its purpose to effect a change in the hearer, to convince or persuade.

(4) A distinctive mark of the parables, what sets them off from other genres of rhetorical literature, is that they convey a teaching which belongs to the sphere of the *religious or ethical.* The Synoptic parables are many and varied, but all express some aspect of Jesus' message about the coming reign of God. They have to do with the following: the breaking-in of the reign of God in history through the ministry of Jesus; the grace of God's reign, or his compassion toward the marginalized and sinners; discipleship, or the challenge to those who would enter into God's reign; and finally the crisis brought on by the imminence of God's reign.

The parables, those striking stories with their lesson so tactfully conveyed, led those who heard them to reflect on Jesus' words, and to bear the responsibility for the decision to accept or reject his claim.

We thus arrive at the following definition of the parable: *every parable is a story; this story conveys a lesson, so that the parable has a double meaning, the story and the lesson; the parable's purpose is to effect a change in the hearer, to lead to decision or action; and the lesson always is religious or moral*. There are, then, four points which define the parable: it tells a story (*narrative*); it has two levels of meaning (*tropical*); its purpose is to persuade, convince, convert (*rhetorical*); and its lesson always has to do with divine and human interrelations (*religious, ethical*). Each of these four points will be more fully spelled out in the next two chapters.

D. The Three Types of Parables

It has been noted, since the late nineteenth century, that the parables in the Gospels fall into three groups. These are usually given the names (1) *similitude*, (2) *parable*, and (3) *exemplary story* (sometimes called *illustration*). It is unfortunate that the word "parable" is thus used in two senses, in the broad sense to refer to all the parables generally, and in the narrow sense to denote one of the three types of parables. The resulting confusion is often deplored, but as yet no other term for the narrower type has been widely adopted.

All of the parables, that is, all three types, have this in common, that they present an implied comparison between an experience or event from ordinary, everyday life, and a reality of the moral or religious order. The characteristics which distinguish each type from the other two are here described, and will be explained in greater depth in the following chapters.

1. Similitude

The similitude is the most concise type of parable. It briefly narrates a typical or recurrent event from real life. It tells a story which everyone would recognize as a familiar experience. Since it has to do with the recurrent or typical, the similitude is usually told in the present tense, although the past tense is occasionally used. The similitude gains its persuasiveness by recounting what is widely recognized as true. No one, on hearing a similitude, is likely to deny that this is the way life is. Such is how anyone would rejoice on finding a lost coin (Lk 15:8-10); this is how seed always grows to full harvest (Mk 4:26-29). Many of the similitudes in Luke's Gospel begin, "Which of you?" (e.g. Lk 11:5; 14:28, 31), "Or what woman?" (Lk 15:8), "Or what king?" (Lk 14:31). Those in the Gospels of Mark and Matthew often begin by stating the comparison: "The kingdom of God is as if" (e.g. Mk 4:26, 30–31; Mt 13:33). Some twelve similitudes appear in the Synoptic Gospels.

Two examples of this type of parable are the following similitudes of the Lost Coin and the Growing Seed. In the first, God's love for the sinner is compared to the homely experience of a poor woman seeking and finding one lost coin, and celebrating with her friends. The interpretation in Luke's Gospel (v. 10) makes explicit the story's meaning:

> [8]Or what woman, having ten silver coins, if she loses one coin, does not light a lamp and sweep the house and seek diligently until she finds it? [9]And when she has found it, she calls together her friends and neighbors, saying, 'Rejoice with me, for I have found the coin which I had lost.' [10]Just so, I tell you, there is joy before the angels of God over one sinner who repents.
>
> (Lk 15:8-10)

In the similitude of the Growing Seed, the coming of the reign of God is compared to the grain's ripening to harvest, a natural occurrence familiar to anyone living in farm country, and yet a mysterious and wonderful event:

> [26]And he said, "The kingdom of God is as if a man should scatter seed upon the ground, [27]and should sleep and rise night and day, and the seed should sprout and grow, he knows not how. [28]The earth produces of itself, first the blade, then the ear, then the full grain in the ear. [29]But when the grain is ripe, at once he puts in the sickle, because the harvest has come."
>
> (Mk 4:26-29)

2. *Parable*

The parable is often (though not always) longer and more detailed than the similitude. The parable tells a story, not about something recurrent in real life, but about a one-time event which is fictitious. While the parables are fictitious, however, they never indulge in the fanciful or fantastic, but remain true-to-life. They derive their persuasiveness from being told in a simple, vivid and fresh way which engages the hearer. Though the Gospels do not use these words, the parables are "once upon a time" stories. They are usually narrated in the past tense. Typical beginnings are these: "There was a rich man" (Lk 16:1); "A certain creditor had two debtors" (Lk 7:41); "A sower went out to sow" (Mk 4:3; Mt 13:3; Lk 8:5). In Matthew's Gospel, however, we again find the beginning which explicitly states the comparison: "The kingdom of heaven may be compared to" (see Mt 13:24; 18:23; 20:1; 22:2). Approximately sixteen of the parables in the Synoptic Gospels belong to the type called *parable* (in the narrow sense).

Examples of this type are the Persistent Widow and the Two Sons, two of the briefer parables. The Persistent Widow has to do with God's liberation of his chosen ones from injustice, need, oppression:

> **18** And he told them a parable, to the effect that they ought always to pray and not lose heart. 2 He said, "In a certain city there was a judge who neither feared God nor regarded man; 3and there was a widow in that city who kept coming to him and saying, 'Vindicate me against my adversary.' 4For a while he refused; but afterward he said to himself, 'Though I neither fear God nor regard man, 5yet because this widow bothers me, I will vindicate her, or she will wear me out by her continual coming.' " 6And the Lord said, "Hear what the unrighteous judge says. 7And will not God vindicate his elect, who cry to him day and night? Will he delay long over them? 8I tell you, he will vindicate them speedily. Nevertheless, when the Son of man comes, will he find faith on earth?"
>
> (Lk 18:1-8)

The parable of the Two Sons is spoken in the temple to religious leaders, the chief priests and the elders (Mt 21:23). Jesus says to them:

> [28]What do you think? A man had two sons; and he went to the first and said, 'Son, go and work in the vineyard today.' [29]And he answered, 'I will not,' but afterward he repented and went. [30]And he went to the second and said the same; and he answered, 'I go, sir,' but did not go.
> (Mt 21:28-30)

Jesus asks his hearers which son did the father's will, and when they reply, "The first," he pronounces this conclusion: "Truly, I say to you, the tax collectors and the harlots go into the kingdom of God before you" (v. 31).

3. Exemplary Story

The exemplary story, like the similitude and parable, presents an implied comparison between an event (real or imagined) drawn from life and a reality of the moral or religious order. The distinction lies in this: The similitude and parable present an analogy between two very different things (e.g. the reign of God is compared to seed, a sinner to a lost coin). The exemplary story presents, not an analogy, but an example, one specific case which illustrates a general principle (e.g. the good Samaritan illustrates love of neighbor in Lk 10:29-37; the tax collector stands for the humble and repentant sinner in Lk 18:9-14; the rich man exemplifies those with materialistic concerns in Lk 16:19-31). In the similitude and parable the two things compared are dissimilar, whereas in the exemplary story they are similar. The exemplary stories resemble the parables (rather than the similitudes) in these respects, that they are fictitious and somewhat developed stories told in the past tense. We find only four similitudes in the Synoptics, all in the Gospel of Luke: the Good Samaritan (Lk 10:29-37); the Rich Fool (Lk 12:16-21); the Rich Man and Lazarus (Lk 16:19–31); and the Pharisee and the Tax Collector (Lk 18:9–14).

Perhaps the most beautiful and best known of the exemplary stories is the Good Samaritan. Jesus tells this story, according to Luke, in response to the lawyer's question, "Who is my neighbor?"

> [30]A man was going down from Jerusalem to Jericho, and he fell among robbers, who stripped him and beat him, and departed, leaving him half dead. [31]Now by chance a priest was going down that road; and when he saw him he passed by on the other side. [32]So likewise a Levite, when he came to the place and saw him, passed by on the other side. [33]But a Samaritan, as he journeyed, came to where he was; and when he saw him, he had compassion, [34]and went to him and bound up his wounds, pouring on oil and wine; then he set him on his own beast and brought him to an inn, and took care of him. [35]And the next day he took out two denarii and gave them to the innkeeper, saying, 'Take care of him; and whatever more you spend, I will repay you when I come back.'
>
> (Lk 10:30-35)

The lawyer grants, when Jesus questions him, that of the three passers-by the Samaritan alone "proved neighbor to the man." Jesus concludes: "Go and do likewise" (vv. 36-37).

2. THE PARABLE AS LITERATURE: ITS STRUCTURE

THE PARABLE is in the first place a kind of speech. All speeches are constructed of the same material, namely words (that is, sounds that are meaningful). But many different kinds of interesting and beautiful constructs can be crafted out of words. I shall now try to show precisely what kind of verbal artifact we have in a parable. In this chapter we shall examine the *structure* of the parable (what it is), and in the next chapter its *purpose or function* (what it does) and its *meaning* (what it says).

A. The Narrative Form

The subject of this section is the parable's *form*. There are only three different forms of speech. (1) One is *expository* speech, or discourse, such as we have in an essay or a descriptive passage. This book is itself an example of discursive or expository writing. In exposition we have speech which is about (abstract) ideas or (concrete) things. Since it has to do with ideas or things rather than action, exposition is a static form of speech. (2) Another form is *narrative*, that is, the form of story-telling, such as we have in short stories, novels, fairy tales, fables, and parables. Narrative always has to do with action or events. It is therefore a dynamic form of speech. (3) The last form is the *dramatic*, such as we have in a dialogue or play. Drama is distinct from narrative in having several speakers. Like narrative, however, drama has to do with action or event, and so is also dynamic. Since both (2) narrative and (3) drama tell stories and are dynamic, a term sometimes employed to include both is *narratory*.

Parables, as we observed earlier, belong to (2) the *narrative* or story form, and so they are dynamic compositions. We have seen that they derive their material from real life, from the everyday world of family and friends, work and worship. They are always drawn from the experiences of Jesus and his audience. The parables, for the most part, have their setting in the rural life of Israel.

Specifically, the parables belong to popular or folk literature. Originally they were not written down at all, but were told orally. They therefore had to be simple enough to be readily understood on hearing, and to be easily remembered afterward. These little stories, then, are very economically told. They are so concise that only what bears on the comparison is narrated. Everything that would distract the listener from the point of comparison is omitted. One might say that the parables are drawn in bold lines and painted in primary colors.

Rudolf Bultmann, in his brilliant work on form criticism, *The History of the Synoptic Tradition*, pointed out the stylistic characteristics of the parable. The following is a summary of his observations.

In a parable, the story is told from a single perspective. Only one scene, that is, one set of events, is narrated. We are not told what is happening off-scene. These terse stories are developed deftly by means of action and speech (both monologue and dialogue).

A parable has no more than two or three chief characters, as for example the widow and the judge (Lk 18:1-8), the father and his two sons (Mt 21:28-32). No characters unessential to the plot appear—no mother in the Prodigal Son (Lk 15:11-32), for instance. Instead of individual characters, there may be groups. In this case, a group is treated as though it were a single character: the invited guests in the Great Feast (Mt 22:2-10; Lk 14:15-24), the laborers in the Laborers in the Vineyard (Mt 20:1-16), the maidens in the Ten Maidens (Mt 25:1-13). They are differentiated only to the extent necessary: for example, those invited to the feast who make excuses, the laborers hired at different hours, the wise and the foolish maidens. Subsidiary characters, as for example the wounded man in the Good Samaritan (Lk 10:29-37), are not described at all.

Only two persons or groups speak or act in one scene. Others remain in the background. If a chief character (for example, the father in the Prodigal Son) speaks to more than one other character (the prodigal son, the elder son), he does so in successive scenes.

Persons are usually characterized by what they say or do, as for example the widow, the two very different sons, and the priest, Levite and Samaritan, or by what others say of them, as when the king calls his servant "wicked" in the Unmerciful Servant (Mt 18:23-35). (Only seldom are attributes explicitly mentioned in the narrative, an instance being the description of the judge as one "who neither feared God nor regarded man" in Lk 18:2.) Similarly, the characters' motives and feelings are rarely described, since they are irrelevant. Thus we are not told why the prodigal son asks for his share of the inheritance and journeys to a far country. They are mentioned only when essential to the story, as when it is said of the father that he "had compassion."

A stylistic device characteristic of folk stories, since they are recounted orally, is repetition. The prodigal son, for instance, confesses twice. Sometimes we have triple repetition, as when three groups of persons invited to the feast make excuses. Repetition is an aid to understanding and to remembrance.

Another device, on which the meaning of several parables is based, is contrast, as between the priest and Levite and the Samaritan, the Two Builders (Mt 7:24-27; Lk 6:47-49), and the Pharisee and the Tax Collector (Lk 18:9-14).

This, then, describes the *form* of the parable, the story itself, which is its literal level of meaning.

B. The Tropical Mode of Meaning

The subject of this section is the *mode of meaning* of the parable. This is an exceedingly important topic, which deserves careful attention. The discussion presented here has as its aim to shed light on a basic issue in the study of parables. Its purpose is to unravel the difficult problem of the relation of parable and allegory. One of the statements most frequently made about parables, and one of the most incorrect and misleading, is the assertion that parables are not allegories. Since the nineteenth century, it has been customary to begin books about parables by setting parable and allegory over against each other as radically different kinds of speech; that fundamental error has clouded the study of parables. A careful reading of what follows here will, it is hoped, help to make clear the definitions of parable and allegory and their relation to each other.

This section is also important because it helps to illuminate a second matter which, as we shall see, is related to the first: this is the interesting tradition which we find in the Bible of regarding the parables as "mysterious" speech. (See Mark 4.) This subject will be discussed later, but the groundwork is laid here.

Tropical Meaning

In all speech, there are only two possible *modes, or kinds, of meaning*: (1) *literal* meaning, and (2) *tropical* meaning. Literal meaning is familiar to all and requires no explanation here. Though the word "tropical" (trope-ical) may be unfamiliar, its sense is quite well known to everyone. It is what we often call "figurative" meaning. "Tropical," the more accurate term, is used in this book. Tropical meaning is meaning in addition to the literal.

Every parable without exception has *both* levels of meaning. As noted earlier, no parable is told simply for the story; it is always intended to convey a message. The direct, literal meaning is the story: it is present in the words themselves, or *explicit*. The indirect, tropical meaning is its message or point: it is not stated in the words of the story, it is important to observe, but is only *implicit*, or suggested indirectly. The hearer must deduce the lesson from the story. (Sometimes the lesson is stated in an interpretation *following* the story; but that is another matter.) To illustrate: The similitude of the Growing Seed (Mk 4:26–29) is on the literal level a little narrative about the ripening of seed to harvest, on the tropical level a lesson about the mysterious but certain coming of the reign of God. The parable of the Prodigal Son (Lk 15:11–32) is on the literal level a story about a lost son's return home to his father, on the tropical level a lesson about God's loving mercy toward the repentant sinner.

It should be emphasized at this point that tropical meaning is only suggested or implied meaning. Again, it is not present in the words themselves, but must be inferred by the hearer. Tropical meaning, therefore, is not necessarily as clear and definite as literal meaning. A tropical composition may or may not be lucid. The interpretation of a tropical composition is sometimes (though not always) subject to debate.

Trope

To explain adequately the tropical meaning of the parables, it is necessary to begin by defining the word "trope." A trope (*tropē* in Greek) is a turn, or change, or play on the meaning of words. It always involves double meaning. A trope occurs in small units of meaning, in one or a few words.

"Trope" is a very broad term. It includes a wide variety of types. Metaphor, synecdoche, metonymy, and irony are only a few of the many kinds of tropes. Since the tropes most often at play in the parables are metaphor and synecdoche, only these two will be defined here.

A *metaphor* is a word (or a few words) having two levels of meaning, the literal meaning and another implied meaning. To borrow an example from Aristotle, a story-teller may, in speaking of Achilles the warrior, say of him, "The lion rushed forward." The word "lion" is a metaphor. It has two meanings: the literal, which is the species of animal, lion; and the tropical, Achilles. The name "Achilles" *does not appear in the sentence;* it is only implied, that is, indirectly meant, by the word "lion." (The hearer or reader would have to deduce from the context that Achilles was meant by the word "lion.") Put another way, in this sentence the lion *stands for* Achilles. What we have in a metaphor is an implied comparison between two very different things. In this metaphor, Achilles, a man, is implicitly compared to something quite different and unexpected, a lion, because he shares with the beast such qualities as courage and strength. We find an abundance of metaphors in the Gospels, as in the saying, "go rather to the lost sheep of the house of Israel" (Mt 10:6) where "sheep" is a metaphor for the Jewish people.

We might note that Aristotle said that of the various ornaments of speech "by far the greatest thing is the use of metaphor. That alone cannot be learned; it is the token of genius. For the right use of metaphor means a perception of the similarity in dissimilar things" (*Poetics* XXII.16-17).

Synecdoche is another type of trope. In synecdoche, as in all tropes, we have two levels of meaning. Thus in synecdoche, too, one word *stands for* another. In this case, the part stands for the whole, the singular for the plural, the individual for the class, and the like. Synecdoche may also be the opposite of these, the greater standing for the lesser. We employ synecdoche when we say, "The Roman won the day," in which the Roman (singular) stands for the Romans (plural) or the Roman army; or when we say "hands" for workers; or "sails" for ships. An interesting biblical example frequently on our lips is "our daily bread," in which bread stands for all our sustenance, and not just bread in the literal sense. It is easy to see the double meaning in this example: "bread" means both bread (literally) and sustenance in general (tropically).

Tropical Stories

It was said above that a trope occurs in small units of speech, in one or a few words. But the very same phenomenon of double meaning can occur also in large units of speech, in whole literary compositions. Any one of the tropes can be extended in such a way that it occurs across an entire story. What happens in a single word in a trope, that is, the double meaning, simply occurs over a broader area, across the entire narratory composition. It will be recalled that the word *narratory* includes both *narrative* and *dramatic* works; any narratory work can have the double-meaning effect. When two levels of meaning are present across an entire work, we say that the whole work is tropical.

Allegory

We are now prepared to formulate a correct definition of allegory. Perhaps no single thing can contribute more to a clear understanding of the parable as a literary construct.

When a *metaphor*, the most common and beautiful of the tropes, is extended across a whole narratory composition, we call the story *allegory*. *The definition of allegory, then, is simply an extended metaphor in narratory form.*

Perhaps the most important point to grasp in our definition is that it says *extended* metaphor—and *not* series of metaphors. I emphasize this because the *mis*understanding of allegory as a series of metaphors, which has unfortunately become lodged in New Testament scholarship, confuses the study of parables. (It is often said, for example, that the Gospel of Mark treats the Sower in 4:3-9,14-20 as an allegory because it interprets the four different kinds of soils as a series of metaphors for four different kinds of hearers of the word; such a view is incorrect.) It must be made clear, therefore, that allegory is metaphor extended across the broad, whole meaning of a story. Whether or not there are also metaphors in the small, constituent meanings (one or a few words) is quite irrelevant; it is not this that constitutes it as an allegory. What makes an allegory is metaphorical meaning across the *whole*.

Metaphor can be extended across any narratory work, that is, any narrative or dramatic composition. It is helpful to use the term as an adjective, and to speak of "allegorical" works. We have allegorical short stories (for example, Hawthorne's "Young Goodman Brown"), allegorical novels (Golding's *Lord of the Flies*), and allegorical plays (*Everyman*). What is of most interest to us is that we also have allegorical similitudes and parables.

Allegory is not, then, a literary genre or form; it is simply a device of meaning (extended metaphor) which can appear in any narratory composition. It is therefore not logical to speak of parable and allegory as though they were two different and mutually exclusive literary genres or forms. Parable *is* a literary genre in itself; allegory is not. Allegory is simply an element (a device of meaning) which may or may not be employed in the making of a parable or other story.

Similitude and Parable as Allegorical (Extended Metaphor)

Since every similitude and parable (in the narrow sense) has both a literal and a metaphorical meaning, every similitude or parable is allegorical. That is to say, the similitude and parable are *extended* metaphors (not series of metaphors). A few examples should suffice to show that this is so. The similitude of the Two Builders (Mt 7:24-27; Lk 6:47-49) is literally a story about two men who build houses, one on rock, the other on sand, and metaphorically (i.e. allegorically) an exhortation to hear and do Jesus' word, and not to hear it only. The parable of the Pearl (Mt 13:45-46) is literally a tale about a merchant who finds a pearl of great value and sells everything he has to buy it, and metaphorically (i.e. allegorically) a lesson about the good news of the reign of God, which leads one to count all else as worthless. The parable of the Unmerciful Servant (Mt 18:23-35) is literally a narrative about a man whose master had released him of his heavy debt out of pity, but who in turn refused to remit the debt of a servant who owed him much less, and metaphorically (i.e. allegorically) an exhortation to forgive others as God forgives us.

Exemplary Story as Extended Synecdoche

It is important now to make clear the following point: if some parables are allegorical, not every parable is so. While allegory may go into the creation of a parable, it does not have to.

It has been pointed out that four parables are set apart from the rest and given the name exemplary story. These are all from the Gospel of Luke: the Good Samaritan (10:29-37); the Rich Fool (12:16-21); the Rich Man and Lazarus (16:19-31); and the Pharisee and the Tax Collector (18:9-14). The tropical meaning employed in these parables is extended synecdoche (and not extended metaphor, i.e. allegory). They are based on the extension of the synecdoche, which is the part for the whole, the one for the many. What is presented in these stories is one particular example to illustrate a general principle—hence the name exemplary story or illustration. In the Good Samaritan, for instance, we are given one specific example which illustrates beautifully the central teaching of Jesus, that "there is no other commandment greater than these," the double commandment to love God and neighbor (Mk 12:28-34; Mt 22:34-40; Lk 10:25-28). In the Pharisee and the Tax Collector, we are given a single example which illustrates strikingly the Gospel theme of reversal of conditions, summarized in the interpretation following the parable: "every one who exalts himself will be humbled, but he who humbles himself will be exalted" (Lk 18:14).

Summary

It was said in Chapter 1 that the similitude and parable on the one hand and the exemplary story on the other are distinguished by this, that the former present an analogy whereas the latter presents an example. It should now be clear why this is so: the similitude and parable are extended metaphors, to which we give the name allegory; the exemplary story is extended synecdoche. (The similitude, it will be recalled, is distinguished from the other two insofar as it narrates something typical or recurrent in real life, rather than a fictitious event.)

As was observed earlier, any of the tropes (metaphor, synecdoche, metonymy, irony, and the rest) may be extended over a whole narratory composition. It happens that a name has been given to the extended metaphor, namely, allegory. Other extended tropes have not been given a name. This is simply an accident of nomenclature. It should not obscure the fact that every kind of trope is equally a trope and every kind of trope can be extended over an entire literary work. Thus the parables that are allegorical and the parables that are extended synecdoches are equally tropical. I stress this point because it is often said that while similitudes and parables are figurative (i.e. tropical) stories, exemplary stories are literal stories. This is simply incorrect. No parable is only literal; all three types are equally tropical.

Every parable without exception, then, has a double meaning across the whole; that is, every parable is tropical in structure. Some parables are allegorical (similitudes, parables), some are not (exemplary stories). But *all* parables are tropical.

The tropical meaning in a parable, then, extends across the large unit of meaning, the whole. What of the small units of meaning, the parts which constitute the whole? These may or may not be tropes. Some parables have several tropes in the small units or constituent meanings; others have few or perhaps even none. The narrator may use tropes in the small meanings on the way to creating the whole parable, but does not have to. Again, it is double meaning across the whole, and not double meaning in the small units, that constitutes a story as tropical.

Finally, what is true of all tropical narratives is true of parables: their meaning may or may not be plain. It is largely the tropical character of the parables that gives rise to debates among exegetes as to the proper interpretation of some of them.

3. THE PARABLE AS LITERATURE: ITS PURPOSE AND MEANING

CHAPTERS 2 AND 3 have as their aim to provide an accurate description of the kind of literary work (or verbal artifact) we have in a parable. In Chapter 2 we examined the *structure* of the parable (what it is). Now in Chapter 3 we shall examine its *function or purpose* (what it does) and its *meaning* (what it says). We shall then be prepared to formulate a concise *definition* of the parable which sums up what has been said in these two chapters.

A. The Art of Rhetoric

The subject of this section is the *function or purpose* of the parable. Speech can be organized in different ways according to the different purposes which it is intended to serve. That is, like all artifacts, speech is always produced for a certain end. There are four different kinds of speech, each having a particular goal.

(1) The first kind of speech is *ordinary conversation or common prose,* such as we employ every day, the purpose of which is simply to communicate. (2) The second kind is *scien-*

tific prose, such as we have in a scholarly article or book, the purpose of which is to communicate knowledge or logical meaning.

Of far greater interest to us are the other two kinds of speech, both of which belong to what we call *"literature,"* or artistic speech. (3) We have already been introduced to the third kind. This is *rhetoric,* which is literary prose. Rhetorical speech has as its purpose to convince or persuade. It is the kind of speech we have, for example, in sermons, in political speeches, and in many novels and short stories. *It is to this kind of speech that the parable belongs,* as pointed out in Chapter 1. (4) Fourth, we have *poetic or aesthetic* speech. The purpose of poetry, which consists of aesthetic patterns of sound and meaning, is to be contemplated or enjoyed by the reader or hearer.

It should be noted at this point that these four ways of organizing speech are not mutually exclusive. No speech has only one of these kinds of organization to the absolute exclusion of the other three. In fact, all four kinds of organization are found, to a greater or lesser degree, in any individual instance of speech. What occurs is that one of them is dominant, and the others more or less subordinate to it. It is the dominant kind of organization that gives its character to a speech, so that we can identify the speech as ordinary or common, scientific, rhetorical, or poetic. Then, a rhetorical speech, for example, could have about it some poetic or aesthetic features, though these would always remain subordinate to the rhetorical character of the whole speech. This is true, for example, of some novels and short stories, as well as of some parables.

It is important to observe, again, that *literature* is a broad term, and that it comprises the last two kinds of speech, poetry and rhetoric (or literary prose). A further point must be made. Both rhetoric and poetry are artistic speech, to which we give the name "literature"; but while poetry is a fine art, rhetoric is a practical art. Rhetoric is the artistic arrangement of language in such a way that it will achieve the goal of persuasiveness, of moving the addressee to decision or action. Rhetoric, then, is intended primarily to serve a social purpose. There are counterparts to this distinction in the other arts. In the visual arts, for example, we have the fine art of painting and the practical art of architecture. An edifice, while it may be a splendid work of art, always serves primarily a practical or social purpose (whether it be a church, a home, a city hall); so it is with rhetoric.

We sometimes read that the parables are poetic or aesthetic; this is quite untrue. The parables are literature, to be sure, but they are not aesthetic or poetic—for their purpose is never solely to be enjoyed or contemplated by the hearer. Their purpose rather is to effect a change of mind or heart in the hearer. If there are aesthetic features in a parable at all, they are subordinate to the parable's rhetorical function; they are there only to serve the rhetorical purpose. The parables, then, are literature, but they belong to rhetoric rather than to poetic. Or, they are works of art, but they belong to a practical rather than to a fine art.

We shall now examine more closely the way in which the Synoptic parables functioned in their original setting, when first uttered by Jesus to his audience. This subject has been explored by Eta Linnemann in her insightful study, and more recently by Jacques Dupont, who adopts and develops her views. What follows here is in large part a summary of their discussions.

A principle of interpretation of the parables held by many exegetes (for example, Dodd, Jeremias, and the two mentioned above), and no doubt a sound one, is that we must set the Gospel parables in their original context in Jesus' ministry (insofar as that is possible) in order properly to comprehend them. When we make an effort to look at the parables in this way, the most basic and important thing we observe is that Jesus addressed many of them, though perhaps not all, to groups of people who saw things differently from him. Jesus sometimes, though not always, used the parables as a means of *dialogue* between himself and persons who held a different view. The task before us now is to specify as precisely as possible the sort of dialogue that must have taken place.

To arrive at an understanding of how Jesus employed the parables, it is helpful first to consider ways in which he did *not* employ them. Some interpreters have understood Jesus' parables as a means of instruction or teaching. The parables' purpose would have been to lay down general maxims, or to illuminate some difficult matter. They would have been used to explain the unknown by the known, or abstract truths by concrete images. This view is no longer widely held. It is generally agreed that Jesus' aim in using parables was not primarily to convey general religious or ethical truths. Another way to state this conclusion is to say that the parables are far more rhetorical than scientific (the kind of speech to which teaching or instruction belongs).

Other scholars, notably Joachim Jeremias, have understood the parables as weapons of controversy. By their means, they say, Jesus either defended himself against criticism from adversaries, or himself attacked his adversaries' views. The parables would have served to reduce the opponents' position to absurdity. Linnemann and Dupont have shown, however, that Jesus was not a combatant, and that, with rare exceptions, he did not use the parables as weapons of warfare for defense or attack. Had he used them in this way, the parables would have accomplished nothing except to silence the adversaries and harden them in their opposition to Jesus. Most important, they would have failed to address the underlying cause of the controversy. This could hardly be a fair description of the method or purpose of Jesus.

Jesus' purpose in speaking in parables, then, was neither to convey information nor to enter into debate. We arrive at an understanding of the parable as having a more definite and more positive purpose: Jesus' goal was to win over his audience to his view. The parable was an earnest gesture on the part of Jesus toward the audience. It was a speech-act which truly involved speaker and hearer in communication. The parables were instruments of genuine *dialogue* between

Jesus and his audience. Jesus' aim was to engage his hearers' attention, to gain their assent, to enable them to adopt his view of things.

The parable, then, is a means of dialogue. Jesus not only presents his own perception of things in the parable; he also anticipates the objections of the listeners. The subject of the parable is the matter itself on which Jesus and his audience hold different views. As Linnemann says, it provides a bridge over the chasm of opposition. The decision to go over to Jesus' side can only be made by the hearers; but Jesus offers the possibility.

The parable moves away from the sensitive and controversial issue, the religious or moral question, and onto fresh terrain— a story. The story, taken from ordinary experience, does not at first resemble too obviously the matter at issue; the parable thus avoids provoking a defensive reaction in the hearers. Often the parable does, however, reflect the two points of view. This is especially evident in the parables which present two contrasting characters or groups; one of these represents Jesus' viewpoint, and we may suppose the other stands for the audience's. The hearer is drawn into the story. As it develops, the view of Jesus emerges as preferable to the other. The audience is invited to take sides, and indeed to adopt the narrator's viewpoint. The hearer is thus led to see things from a fresh perspective. The parable then moves from the story level to the religious or ethical subject under discussion. The parable has made it possible for the hearer's mind to be opened to new understanding.

Dupont addresses the question how the parables achieve their persuasive power. They do not derive their persuasiveness, he says, from logical argument. Neither do they base it on the authority of quotations from Scripture (the Old Testament), as do many of the rabbinic parables. They owe their effectiveness to their appeal to experience, either the common experience of the audience, or the unique experience of Jesus. In the former case the hearer, recognizing in the story that this is how life is, may be led to a fresh view of things (as for example in the Lost Sheep, Mt 18:12-

14; Lk 15: 3–7). This is clearly how those parables are intended to function which have a beginning such as "Which of you?" (e.g. Lk 11:5; 14: 28, 31; 15:8). In the latter case, the compelling presentation of Jesus' experience may lead the hearer to adopt his view (as in the Great Feast, Mt 22: 2–10; Lk 14: 15–24).

Some interpreters of the parables have employed the term *language event* to describe what occurs in the parabolic speech-act. The parable, a challenge, compels a decision. It creates the possibility of new understanding, of an altering of the situation in which the hearer is enabled to view things from the speaker's perspective, the possibility of conversion and new life. But even if the hearer persists in the old view, a decision has been made, and the situation is not unaltered, for the position becomes one of explicit opposition.

B. The Religious Genre

The subject of this section is the *genre* of the parable. Genre is a classification based on the meaning in a work, that is, its subject, or what it says. There are, as we have seen, only three basic types of literary form; there are only two possible modes of meaning in all speech; and there are only four divisions of speech with respect to the ends for which it is produced. There are, however, as many genres as there are subjects about which one can speak or write. The list of genres is limitless. The genre of a work, again, is determined by the subject to which it refers—for example, heroes in epic, shepherds in pastoral, the comic in comedy, the serious in tragedy. The parables of Jesus, as we observed, belong to the genre of *religious* literature.

The meaning of the parables will be discussed in further detail in Part Two of this book, in which the Synoptic parables are interpreted. In this section, only the major themes of the parables as a whole are outlined.

Dupont has made some interesting observations on the

meaning or subject of the parables, which I here summarize. He points out that the parables have to do with action or events, rather than with ideas or theory; they are, then, dynamic. We have already noted that the literal level of the parable, the story, belongs to the narrative form, which is dynamic reference to event or action. Dupont goes further, maintaining that the parable's subject, what we have designated its tropical meaning, is also dynamic. The parables are not about abstract truths, which are quite properly the subject of systematic theology. The parables are not expositions of truths; they are, rather, narratives about praxis, about either the behavior of the hearers or the actions of God or Jesus. They do not speak, for example, of divine attributes, of what God is, but of how God acts. The dynamic character of the parables points up the fact that the reign of God is not a state (not static), but an event, something happening or becoming (i.e. dynamic), into which the hearer is invited to enter.

To underline a point made by Dupont: by and large the parables have to do with interrelations and interaction. They speak of God's attitude and actions toward the hearers, and especially of the implications that has for the hearers' attitude and actions toward God and others.

One possible way to group the parables (though not the only one) is according to four major themes we can discern in them. (1) Some parables have to do with the breaking-in of God's reign in Jesus' ministry and of its coming in the future. In these parables, Jesus asks the hearers to recognize in his ministry—so marked by failures and contradictions—God's action in inaugurating his reign. (2) Other parables have to do with Jesus' fellowship with outcasts and sinners. In these parables, Jesus shows that by his actions he is bringing the grace of God's reign. God's way of acting toward sinners and the helpless in society is also Jesus' way. (3) A large number of parables have as their subject the behavior of the hearers. These have to do with discipleship, with what is required of those who would enter God's reign. (4) Still others issue a warning, an announcement of the impending judgment, and a call to repentance.

C. Summary: The Definition of the Parable

Four aspects of any speech which the literary theorist may examine are its form, mode of meaning, purpose and genre. We have, in Chapters 2 and 3, looked at these four aspects of the parable as speech. What we observed is here summarized.

The first two aspects have to do with the STRUCTURE of the speech. (1) *Form:* there are only three basic types of form in speech, and of these the parable belongs to the *narrative* form. (2) *Mode of meaning:* there are only two possible modes of meaning in all speech, and the parable employs in addition to the literal the *tropical* mode of meaning.

The third aspect has to do with the PURPOSE OR FUNCTION of the speech. (3) *Purpose:* there are four kinds of speech with respect to the purposes for which it is produced, and of these the parable belongs to one of the two types of literature, the practical art of *rhetoric* or literary prose. The fourth aspect has to do with the MEANING of the speech. (4) *Genre:* there is no limit to the number of possible literary genres; the parable belongs to the *religious or moral* genre.

We may define the parable, then, as *a tropical narrative which functions as religious or ethical rhetorical speech.*

A final point must be added. What has been described in Chapters 2 and 3 are the *parables* themselves. A word should be said about the *interpretations* following some of these parables in the Synoptic Gospels. These interpretations belong, like the parables, to rhetorical speech and to the religious genre. They differ from the parables, however, in belonging to the discursive or expository (rather than narrative) form and to the literal (rather than tropical) mode of meaning. A parable is a tropical narrative; its interpretation is literal discourse. (See, for example, the interpretations following the parables of the Two Sons in Mt. 21:31 and of the Lost Sheep and the Lost Coin in Lk 15:7,10.) The interpretation states explicitly what is implicit in the parable itself, namely, its lesson or point.

4. THE MARKAN VIEW OF PARABLES

A. The Problem

IN THE GOSPEL of Mark, chapter 4, we find an interesting but problematic theory about the parables. The theory is taken over with some changes in Matthew 13 and Luke 8. The Markan chapter is by no means an easy passage to interpret, but it is a theologically rich one. Mark's theory has played an important role in the study of parables since the nineteenth century, and it deserves consideration here.

The Markan view is that the parables are somehow "mysterious" speech, that is, difficult for the hearers to comprehend. In the Gospel, Jesus has just spoken the parable of the Sower to a large crowd without elucidating it (4:1-9). Afterward, the disciples "who were about him with the twelve," now alone with Jesus, ask him "concerning the parables" (v. 10). It is at this point that the Markan view of parables is stated:

> [11]And he said to them, "To you has been given the secret [Greek *mystērion*] of the kingdom of God, but for those outside everything is in parables; [12]so that they may indeed see but not perceive, and may indeed hear but not understand; lest they should turn again, and be forgiven."
> (Mk 4: 11–12; adaptation of Isa 6: 9–10 in v. 12)

The disciples themselves had evidently not understood the Sower, for Jesus says to them: "Do you not understand this parable? How then will you understand all the parables?" (v. 13). He then goes on to interpret the Sower for this inner group of followers (vv. 14–20).

The Markan theory, then, involves a division between the inner circle of disciples, who are enlightened, and "those outside," who are left in the dark. We may briefly describe the theory thus: according to Mark, the parables are obscure speech; they have to do somehow with the outsiders' exclusion from understanding (truly seeing and hearing), conversion (turning again), and forgiveness. To explain such a theory of parables certainly presents a challenge to the exegete. A central question posed by the passage is whether it is Jesus who excludes "those outside," or whether they exclude themselves, or whether there is an interaction at work. Before addressing this question, it would be well to summarize and dismiss one explanation commonly given for the Markan view.

Some New Testament interpreters have explained the Markan theory—inaccurately—in the following way. On the lips of the historical Jesus, these stories were parables. The parable is by nature clear speech, which has as its purpose to shed light on a subject. The parable makes only one point, which is always obvious. It therefore requires no interpretation (an opinion which casts doubt on the interpretations accompanying some parables in the Gospels). The parable, then, was suitable for Jesus' use in preaching to the simple, unlettered people of the land. In the hands of Mark, and even of others before him, however, the parables were transformed into a radically different kind of speech, allegories. Allegory is by nature obscure, esoteric speech, intended to disguise a thing. An allegory has many points, and must be interpreted, or decoded. (The mistake made here, as noted earlier, is that allegory is defined incorrectly as a series of metaphors, rather than correctly as an extended metaphor.) It is unmistakable that Jesus could have preached in this way. Mark and others, then, seriously misconstrue the kind of speech Jesus used; this misconception is reflected in Mark 4.

We have already seen that this way of setting parable and allegory over against each other is fundamentally wrong; the relation between parable and allegory was correctly described in Chapter 2. There must therefore be a more sound interpretation than the one outlined above for the Markan view of parables. The explanation advanced here covers three topics: the kind of speech we have in a parable; the parable as employed by the historical Jesus in his ministry; and the parable as employed in the Gospel of Mark. It is important to keep distinct these last two topics, the levels of the historical Jesus and of the Gospel of Mark.

B. Tropical Speech and "Mystery"

The first question before us is this: why is it that the parables were understood as somehow "mysterious" speech by the ancients? The answer is that it is because they employ the tropical mode of meaning. It is the structure of double meaning present in every parable that makes possible its functioning as "mysterious" language. The speaker pronounces the parable. The parable itself has two levels of meaning. The hearer has few difficulties in understanding the story itself, the direct or literal meaning. But what the story in turn suggests, the indirect or tropical meaning, is not always immediately evident. The hearer may miss the lesson or point of the parable, because it is only implied and must be deduced. The hearer may be either unwilling or unable to grasp the parable's lesson. The "mysteriousness," then, consists quite simply in the hearer's unwillingness or inability to understand the indirect and more important level of meaning of the parable. It is precisely because they employ the tropical mode of meaning that the parables are both unusually striking and effective speech, and speech that is not always simple and straightforward to interpret.

All of this is not to say that every parable is difficult to comprehend; that is surely not the case. Many of the parables are quite clear, and are easily grasped on first hearing; others, however, may present difficulties. It is not *necessary* that a parable be difficult to understand; it is *possible*.

The fact that they are tropical gave rise to a tradition in ancient Israel about the character of the parables as obscure speech. This is not the only way of viewing the parables in the Old Testament, but it is well attested. Mark was certainly not the first to understand the parables in such a way. We know from references in the biblical literature that the tradition of regarding the *mashal* or parable as mysterious existed from at least the writing of the books of Samuel and Kings down to the New Testament period. Some of the passages where this view is reflected are 2 Sam 12:1–7; 14:4–13; 1 Kgs 20: 39–42; Ps 78: 2; Sir 39: 2–3; 47: 15. An excellent example is the Old Testament parable quoted in Chapter 1, the parable of the Ewe Lamb, which the prophet Nathan addressed to David (2 Sam 12: 1–7). There the parable is employed as a device to trick the hearer into pronouncing judgment on himself. The stratagem would not work if the parable were perfectly clear; it depends for its marvelous effect on indirect meaning and the hearer's failure to grasp it. Two other Old Testament parables which function in exactly the same way are the wise woman of Tekoa's Two Brothers and the Avengers (2 Sam 14: 4–13) and the anonymous prophet's Escaped Prisoner (1 Kgs 20: 39–42). Mark, then, did not invent the view of the parable as "mysterious"; rather he stood at the end of a long Isrealite tradition. This tradition derived from a sound insight on the part of the ancients regarding parabolic speech.

C. The Use of the Parable in Jesus' Ministry

We come now to the next question: how was the parable employed by Jesus himself during his ministry? Certainly it could not have been Jesus' intention to use parables in order to render his message incomprehensible. We may dismiss that notion out of hand. Yet, as we look at the parables in the Synoptic Gospels, we cannot help but observe that there is variation with respect to how easy or difficult they are to understand. For example, the Growing Seed (Mk 4:26-29) is quite abstruse. The Prodigal Son (Lk 15:11-32) is considerably more lucid. Most parables fall somewhere between these two. Some are quite clear and require little or no explanation; others are obscure enough to need interpretation of some sort. There is no hard and fast rule here.

The first circle of hearers, those who heard the parables from Jesus himself, must have asked, "What does the man mean?" They must have wondered, that is, what his point might be in telling this story. The meaning of a parable would have been conveyed to them in different ways. In some instances, the social situation in which the parable was told, its context, would indicate what the lesson might be. In others, the question or discussion preceding the parable would give the clue to its meaning. Many of the tropes appearing in the Synoptic parables were standard and well known in first-century Judaism. For example, God was often represented as a ruler, a judge, a parent, the owner of a vineyard or field; the people of Israel were depicted as servants, children, a vine or flock; the judgment was represented as a harvest or a reckoning; and God's reign as a feast or wedding. Jesus' audience would immediately have understood these tropes. Perhaps Jesus sometimes gave an interpretation following the parables. We can observe that the parables in the Old Testament and the rabbinic literature are often accompanied by explanations. The rabbis no doubt interpreted their parables explicitly, at least sometimes; there is no reason to believe that Jesus would have employed the parables differently from other rabbis. Thus, in one or all of these ways, the hearers would have been able to grasp the meaning of the story Jesus told.

An observation made by a New Testament scholar writing at the beginning of this century, M.-J. Lagrange, seems to me sound. Noting that the parable is not always absolutely clear, Lagrange explained this by saying that the purpose of a parable is to strike the imagination, to pique the curiosity, to make the listener reflect and work to arrive at the meaning, but only so that the lesson will be more deeply engraved on the mind.

Again, this is not to say that Jesus employed parables with the aim of making his subject obscure. A parable is an implied comparison. The comparison is not always obvious; but once it is perceived it sheds new light on the subject under discussion. The purpose of a parable is to move to decision or action; paradoxically, that purpose is perhaps more effectively achieved precisely because the speaker proceeds indirectly rather than directly.

D. The Use of the Parable in Mark's Gospel

We now address our final question: to what use was the parable put in the Gospel of Mark, written some forty years after the death and resurrection of Jesus? In describing Mark's use of the parable, we are doing in part what is recalled Redaction Criticism. This is the study of the special emphases, motifs and themes, and theological views which each evangelist contributed to the Synoptic material. Each gospel has distinctive literary and theological characteristics; these were placed upon the material by the individual evangelist as he selected and shaped ("redacted") the many stories and sayings he received from the tradition to produce the final literary composition. Redaction Criticism is the examination of these distinctive features. (See the discussion of Redaction Criticism in the introductory volume of this series by Daniel J. Harrington, *Interpreting the New Testament*.) Again, it is necessary to keep distinct Jesus' use of the parable and Mark's; they are not in every respect identical.

Mark is often charged in the scholarly literature with distorting the parable as a verbal construct, that is, with taking clear parabolic speech and transforming it into obscure allegorical speech; this charge is simply unfounded. Rather, Mark has taken what is essential to the parable, the double-meaning effect, and put it to the service of a theological theme of mystery, an important feature of the Second Gospel. But Mark's notion of mystery must be carefully described: it has to do, not with the audience's intellectual imperceptiveness, but with its resistance to accepting the message of Jesus. In Mark's Gospel, the hearers' failure to understand the parables has much more to do with unwillingness than with inability. We see this, for example, in Mk 4:13, where Jesus asks the disciples concerning the Sower: "Do you not understand this parable? How then will you understand all the parables?" The question clearly infers that the hearers can and should comprehend the parabolic preaching of Jesus. The "mystery" of the parable is a mystery, not of intellectual obtuseness, but of spiritual obduracy—what the Bible calls "hardness of heart" (see Mk 3:5; 6:52; 8:17; 10:5). Although the term "hardness of heart" does not appear in Mk 4:10-13, the concept is present; it is expressed by the notions of spiritual blindness and deafness. (The term "hardness of heart" does appear in Isa 6:10, which is quoted in Mk 4:12, and in Jn 12:40, where the same passage from Isaiah is quoted.) In the Bible, blindness, deafness and hardness of heart are equivalent terms for obduracy; their opposites are faith and repentance. (See e.g. Isa 6:9-10; Ezek 2:4-5,7; 3:7; Mk 8:17-18.)

In Mark, understanding is not so much knowledge as faith and obedience; and incomprehension is not a matter of intellectual obtuseness but of hardness of heart. We have here not a mystery of dogma, but a mystery of application or appropriation. The parables are about the implications of the coming reign of God for the situation of the audience. Mark's theory is that the meaning of the parables is perceived only by those disposed to accept Jesus' preaching about the coming reign of God and the requirements made of the hearers. In the Second Gospel, the mystery has to do with the hearers' refusal to see that in the ministry of Jesus, marked by suffering and failure, the reign of God breaks in, and especially with their refusal to accept the role that suffering may play in their own lives, that is, with the cost of discipleship. As the interpretation of the Sower shows (Mk 4: 14–20), truly to understand the parables means to hear and do them—to accept their message in faith, but more importantly, steadfastly to observe them in one's life in the face of difficulties of all kinds.

It is true that in Mark 4 it would appear to be God who, through the parables, causes "those outside" to be spiritually blind and deaf. That is because in the Bible we often find an interaction between free will and determinism; they are held together in uneasy tension. While the biblical theologians recognized human freedom and moral responsibility, they also recognized God's sovereignty, his absolute control over all history (a belief from which determinism and predestination derive). Consequently it is often difficult if not impossible to decide who ultimately causes the hardening of heart. We have here a theological problem which, it must be conceded, cannot be worked out in accordance with strict logic. The rabbis summed up their view of the matter by saying: "If a man chooses to do good the heavenly powers help him. If he chooses to do evil, they leave the way open to him" (*Babylonian Talmud, Shabbath* 104a). We find the same yoking together of free will and determinism, and the same absence of any attempt to reconcile them, in the Old Testament, the Intertestamental Literature, the rabbinic literature, and the New Testament.

There is a spiritual law at work in the hearing of the word. While the hearer makes the initial decision to see or not to see, to hear or not to hear, God assists the hearer in that choice:

> 24 And he said to them, "Take heed what you hear; the measure you give will be the measure you get, and still more will be given you. 25 For to him who has will more be given; and from him who has not, even what he has will be taken away."
>
> (Mk 4:24-25)

The openness and attentiveness which the hearer brings to

a parable will be the measure of understanding he or she will receive from it. Notions of this kind were well known in Judaism. We read in Daniel, to cite only one example, that God "gives wisdom to the wise and knowledge to those who have understanding" (Dan 2: 21).

The theological theme of mystery in the Second Gospel has a dual purpose. First, with respect to "those outside," the mystery is explained in Mk 4:11–12. The secret of the reign of God is not given to the outsiders because such is not God's plan. A problem remains, however: the identity of "those outside" is not clear. Some exegetes think that they stand generally for all those who, down to Mark's day, had heard the Gospel and rejected it. Other exegetes, however, think that "those outside" stand more specifically for the Jews. They believe that Mark 4 deals with what was a difficult problem for early Christians, namely, the historical fact that the Jewish people by and large had not accepted Jesus as Messiah. Mark explains this by showing that the exclusion of the Jewish people was owing to their resistance to hearing the word, but that it was also part of the broader divine plan—that is, that the Gospel would as a consequence of the rejection by Jews break out of the boundaries of Israel to reach the Gentiles. The same problem is addressed in Romans 9–11 (note especially 9:18; 11:7–8, 25); see also Jn 12:37–40; Acts 28:25–28. Whether "those outside" are all who rejected the Gospel or only the Jewish people, what is distinctive in Mark is his placing of the parables in the service of this early Christian theology regarding those outside the community of believers.

Second, with respect to the inner circle of disciples, the purpose of the mystery may be described as follows. Though the secret of the reign of God is given to them, they, too, fail to apprehend it fully. We see this in Mk 4:13; 6:52; 8:17–18. They are like those in the Markan explanation of the Sower (4:14–20) who are in danger of falling away under pressure of the cares of the world, tribulation and persecution. "Those about him with the twelve" (Mk 4:10) stand for the Christian readers of Mark's Gospel who are being called upon not only to hear, but to hear and faithfully to do the word—for that ultimately is what understanding means.

(See the commentary on Mark by Wilfrid Harrington in this series, and my own detailed discussion of the Markan theory in *The Mysterious Parable: A Literary Study*.)

5. INTERPRETING THE SYNOPTIC PARABLES

A. The Authenticity of the Parables

THE EVENTS of the death and resurrection of Jesus occurred *ca.* A.D. 30; the three Synoptic Gospels were composed some forty to sixty years later. During the intervening decades, narratives about Jesus' deeds and units of his teaching were remembered in the local churches. Recollections of Jesus' ministry existed mostly as individual stories and sayings which were preserved and handed on by word of mouth. It was various materials of this kind which went into the composition of the Synoptic Gospels. Probably the earliest collection of any length was a source we call "Q" (for the German word *Quelle*, "source"); this was comprised mainly of Jesus' sayings, including such important teaching as the Sermon on the Mount, compiled perhaps *ca.* A.D. 50. Next, the Gospel of Mark was written, probably *ca.* A.D. 70; it contains mostly, though not exclusively, stories about Jesus' deeds. Finally, the Gospels of Matthew and Luke were written, *ca.* A.D. 80–90. Both of these were composed—independently of each other—by combining the two sources, Q and Mark, and adding miscellaneous other materials, which we designate "M" (special Matthew, i.e., unique to Matthew) and "L" (special Luke) respectively. Thus the formation of the Synoptic Gospels can be graphically depicted as follows:

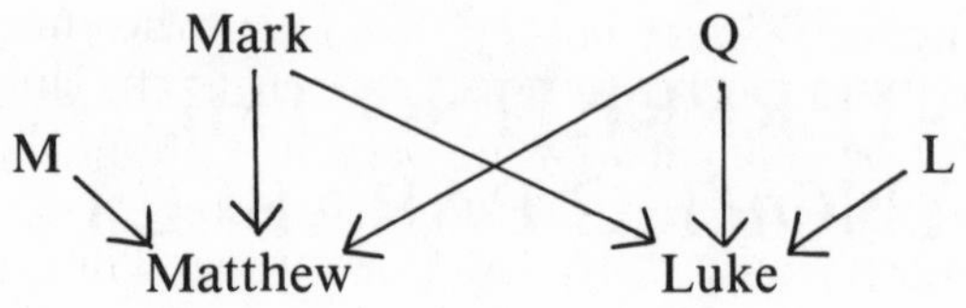

Those parables which appear in all three Synoptic Gospels were for the most part borrowed by Matthew and Luke from Mark. Most of those appearing in both Matthew and Luke (but not in Mark) were taken from Q. Those in Matthew alone we attribute to M, and those in Luke alone to L. For a list of the parables according to their sources, see Appendix II, "The Sources of the Parables."

It is natural that during the period of oral transmission following the death and resurrection of Jesus the Christian communities, as a way of meeting their own needs, made adaptations and modifications in the material, and even contributed new material created by themselves. Finally, each evangelist edited or "redacted" the material he received as he composed his Gospel. A question of great interest to the student of the Gospels, then, is that of the authenticity or historical reliability of the stories and sayings in the Gospels. An element or feature of the Synoptics may be (1) an authentic saying or deed of *Jesus*, or (2) a modification of an authentic element or a creation by the *early Church*, or (3) a modification or a contribution by the *evangelist*, which we call "redaction." (See the chapters on "Source Criticism," "Form Criticism," "Historical Criticism," and "Redaction Criticism" in Daniel J. Harrington, *Interpreting the New Testament*, in this series.)

Interpreters of the New Testament generally regard the parables, taken as a whole, as among the most assuredly authentic sayings of Jesus. The parables express what is most central and characteristic in the message and mission of Jesus. Jesus conducted his ministry both by preaching and by action. There is a remarkable coherence between the words and works of Jesus, reflecting the singleness of his vision; he enacted what he preached about the reign of God. We can discern the main features of Jesus' own understanding of his mission from non-parabolic elements, both sayings and deeds, preserved in the different sources (Q, Mk, M, L). The parables are consistent with what we can learn from these. They express, as does Jesus' entire ministry, a highly distinctive religious view.

In the parables Jesus proclaims the coming of God's reign in the future and—what is astonishingly new and unique in his message—its inauguration in the present through his own ministry. We know that Jesus showed special concern for the sick, the sinners, the poor, the women—for those groups marginalized by society; in the parables he preaches the good news that God's reign brings healing to the afflicted, forgiveness to sinners, and liberation to the oppressed. In the parables, Jesus confronts his hearers with the claims of God's reign and challenges them to decision and action; he lays down for his hearers the requirements of discipleship. He also calls for repentance in view of God's coming reign, warning his hearers of the impending judgment. Throughout the parables we see reflected Jesus' conflict with the religious authorities: he defends himself against their criticism of his association with sinners and other transgressions against the law, and he in turn criticizes their hollow legalism and traditionalism.

The Synoptic parables also reflect the first-century Palestinian Jewish milieu. Both Dodd and Jeremias have shown that they give an accurate and complete picture of the life and customs of the small villages of Palestine, then a province of the Roman Empire. While the New Testament books are written entirely in Greek, we can detect here and there in the Synoptic parables traces of an Aramaic original; this was the living language of first-century Palestine, the mother tongue of Jesus and his contemporaries. While these marks of first-century Palestinian Jewish culture do not prove the authenticity of any of the parables, since they could have come from the Palestinian Christian community, they indicate at the least that the parables are of early, Palestinian origin, which creates a presumption in favor of authenticity.

All of this having been said, it should be added, finally, that each parable must be studied individually and its genuineness assessed on its own merits.

B. Modifications in the Parables

If the parables are by and large authentic teaching of Jesus, however, we must recognize that they are also subjected to changes during the period of oral tradition. They are not, at least not in every case, recorded in the Gospels exactly as they were uttered by Jesus. In this respect they are like all the other forms in the Synoptic Gospels—apophthegms, proverbs, miracle stories, and the rest—which were sometimes modified as they were handed on by word of mouth. In interpreting the parables, therefore, one of the exegete's tasks is to attempt to identify as far as possible what is original and what is secondary (whether from the early Church or the evangelist). The changes which occurred in the parables is discussed extensively by Joachim Jeremias in his masterly work, *The Parables of Jesus*. He treats some ten different kinds of modifications, which he calls "principles of transformation," attributable to the primitive Church and the evangelists. To illustrate such changes, I shall give examples here of only two types of modifications: changes in the setting, that is, the social context in which the parable is spoken, and in the interpretation or application of the parable.

(1) Evidently the setting, the social situation in which a parable was uttered by Jesus, was not as well remembered or as faithfully preserved as the parable itself; consequently it was sometimes changed. The similitude of the Lost Sheep provides a clear illustration of change of this kind; we are in a position to compare its setting in two Gospels, those of Matthew and Luke.

In Luke's Gospel (15:3–6), Jesus addresses the similitude to opponents, the Pharisees and scribes, who criticize his table fellowship with tax collectors and sinners (vv. 1–2). He responds by telling this similitude about a shepherd who rejoices greatly after seeking and finding one lost sheep from his flock of one hundred. The interpretation is explicitly stated: "there will be more joy in heaven over one sinner who repents than over ninety-nine righteous persons who need no repentance" (v. 7). It is because God delights in forgiveness that Jesus associates with sinners. In Luke we very likely have the original setting and meaning of the similitude.

In Matthew's Gospel (18:12–13) we find a different audience. Jesus here addresses the parable to his disciples (v. 1). The verse preceding the similitude is an admonition not to despise "one of these little ones" (v. 10); the verse following it concludes that it is not God's will "that one of these little ones should perish" (v. 14). There follows an instruction concering the discipline of a brother who has sinned (vv. 15–17). In Matthew's Gospel, then, the meaning of the similitude is that church leaders, those responsible for pastoral care, must diligently seek after apostates. Thus the emphasis has shifted from vindication of the good news concerning God's loving forgiveness to an exhortation to community leaders to seek those who have strayed from the community.

This is one example of a general tendency evident in the Synoptic tradition to change the audience from opponents of Jesus to his disciples; this change results, moreover, in a shift in the parables' meaning. The general tendency is owing to the fact that parables originally addressed by Jesus to his adversaries must now be made meaningful to an audience of Christian hearers and readers. This example illustrates the close relation between the social situation in which a parable is spoken and its meaning.

(2) The first generations of Christians, on hearing the parables were, as we have just seen, led to ask how they applied to their own situation. They wondered what message the parables held for them. Hence the parables were sometimes given new interpretations or applications as they were recounted in different settings.

The parable of the Unjust Steward (Lk 16:1–8) is a case in point. To the parable is added not just one but a series of four applications, joined together on the basis of catchwords which appear either in the parable or in the preceding application ("mammon," "prudent," "faithful," "unrighteous" or "unjust"). The parable tells the story of a steward who, being dismissed from his position for having wasted his master's goods, finds himself in a crisis situation. He meets the situation by sending for his master's debtors and having them rewrite their bills for lesser amounts; he would thus be cared for by the debtors in the future. The master commends him for his prudent and resolute action in the face of this crisis (v. 8a). The point of the parable is that the hearers must likewise act prudently and resolutely in the present in view of the future judgment; the parable must then have been addressed originally to a general audience, and not just to the disciples, as in its Lukan context (v. 1).

Then follow the four interpretations. Verse 8b, "the sons of this world are wiser. . .than the sons of light," applies the parable to the Christian audience, exhorting them to decisive action, like that of the steward's, in view of the crisis of the end-time. Verse 9, "make friends for yourselves by means of unrighteous mammon," urges the hearers to use money (perhaps illegally obtained) to help others; if the reference is to almsgiving, we have here an important Lukan motif. Verses 10–12 enjoin faithfulness in the daily use of what is entrusted to one. Verse 13 sets in opposition to each other the service of God and the service of mammon. Thus we see how a parable could gather to itself several different interpretations, even on so simple a basis as catchwords. F.C. Grant and C.H. Dodd have both remarked that we can almost see here notes for separate sermons on the parable as Christian instruction.

Other kinds of changes also occurred: in a few instances, the parables themselves, and not just their settings or interpretations, were modified; in one or two cases, two originally separate parables were conflated, that is, joined together. Thus perhaps the most basic task of the exegete is to recover the original parable and its meaning, as far as possible.

C. Guidelines for Interpretation

The question arises, then, how we are to go about interpreting the Synoptic parables. It should be said at the outset that there is no fool-proof method for arriving at the exact meaning of a parable as originally uttered by Jesus. As has been shown, the parables are tropical speech; their meaning is therefore only indirect, suggested meaning. Tropical meaning is never as clear, definite and fixed as literal meaning. This is not to say, however, that the meaning of the parables eludes us altogether. We can, indeed, arrive at an understanding of most of the parables, as originally spoken by Jesus, with a fair degree of accuracy, and we must simply be willing to settle for something less than absolute precision and certainty in some cases.

The discussion in the scholarly literature of the past century or so as to how to interpret the parables has focused on certain principles of interpretation, which are reducible to three basic guidelines. Following is a brief description and assessment of these guidelines.

(1) The first has to do with the faulty contrast drawn between parable and allegory. In the late nineteenth and early twentieth centuries, it was a widely held principle, but a flawed one, that the parables have one point only, and not

many points, as do allegories. (Again, such a notion stems in large part from the incorrect definition of allegory as a *series* of metaphors, rather than an *extended* metaphor.) On this view, the constituent meanings in the parables, such as the individual characters, have no independent significance. For example, the father, the prodigal son, and the elder son in the Prodigal Son (Lk 15:11–32) have no meaning of their own, that is, they do not stand for anyone. Neither do the priest and Levite, the Samaritan, and the wounded man in the Good Samaritan (Lk 10:29–37). In recent decades, this view has been modified by interpreters; most would now agree that some of the constituent elements in the parables do have independent meaning.

I would suggest that it is more accurate and helpful to speak of the meaning of the *whole* parable and the meaning of its *parts* than to speak of "one point" and "many points." To speak of the whole meaning and the constituent meanings sets the problem in the proper framework. *A parable is always tropical across its whole meaning; it may or may not have tropes also in its small, constituent meanings.* Whether or not there are tropes in the small meanings, the mental process of interpreting a parable is the same. The hearer grasps the literal meaning of the parable, the story, and then perceives that this in turn suggests a further, tropical meaning. Once the whole meaning is apprehended, the small, constituent meanings fall into place; or conversely, once the small, constituent meanings are understood, the meaning of the whole emerges. A parable having several tropes in the small meanings is no more difficult to interpret than one having a few or no tropes at all in the small meanings. (It is certainly not true that the former is a dark allegory, the latter a lucid parable.)

Most of the Synoptic parables do in fact have tropes in the constituent meanings. It is not necessary that this be so; it simply happens to be the case. It is possible for a parable to have many tropes in its constituent elements, or to have few, or even to have none at all. The longer parables, naturally, are apt to have more tropes than those that are shorter; but the difference is negligible. In the Prodigal Son, for instance, the father stands for God, the prodigal son for repentant sinners, and the elder son for those who are righteous. The meaning of the whole parable is that God bestows loving forgiveness upon the sinner who repents. In the Good Samaritan, the priest and Levite represent officials of the established religion, the Samaritan those who stand outside the circle of God's people, and the wounded man anyone in need. The meaning of the whole parable is that it is the concrete deed of love for the neighbor in need, and not merely official, outward religion, that matters before God.

A word of caution should be added. If there are tropes in *some* of the small, constituent meanings of a parable, there are not tropes in *all*. Some restraint is necessary if our interpretations are not to become wildly fanciful. (Such unrestrained interpretation is what exegetes correctly object to when they warn against "allegorizing.") In the Good Samaritan, for instance, the priest and Levite, the Samaritan, and the wounded man have tropical meaning—but not the town of Jericho, the inn, or the innkeeper. To give tropical significance to elements such as these is to depart from the intention of Jesus and merely to indulge one's own imagination. Again, the constituent meanings must be interpreted in the context of the whole meaning.

(2) There is a consensus among interpreters that the parables have to do with specific truths. This view represents a rejection of an assumption common in the late nineteenth century that the parables convey general religious truths applicable in all times and places. Recent interpreters are generally agreed that this earlier view reduced the parables to teachings about religious and ethical commonplaces. For example, the parable of the Talents or Pounds (Mt 25:14–30; Lk 19:11–27), in an earlier generation, was given a broad application; it was understood as an injunction to be faithful in all that God has entrusted to us. More recently, exegetes have understood it as applying

originally—that is, in Jesus' ministry—to a specific group, perhaps to the Pharisees (Dodd), whose exclusive religion prevented them from serving the sinners, the poor, the Gentiles, or to the scribes (Jeremias), to whom had been entrusted the word of God; in either case, the hearers were warned that they would soon have to render an account as to how they had used God's gift.

The principle that the parables have a specific, distinctive point rather than a broad, general message seems to have held up as a sound one after some two decades of practical application. As has frequently been pointed out, the parables can be given a generalizing meaning only if we remove them from their context in Jesus' ministry, or only if we interpret them apart from Jesus' intention. That the parables convey specific lessons remains a reliable guideline for their interpretation.

(3) The third guideline for interpretation, which is closely related to the second, is a disputed one. As just noted, some of the major interpreters of the last few decades, such as Dodd and Jeremias, maintain that in order properly to apprehend the meaning of the parables, we must set them in their context in the ministry of Jesus. The exegete must attempt to reconstruct the situation in which a parable was first uttered, and to determine the ideas both of Jesus and of his audience, in order correctly to interpret it; where the specific situation is beyond recovery, we may situate the parable in Jesus' ministry as a whole. In recent years, other interpreters have questioned this principle, arguing that the parables can and should be detached from their setting in the ministry of Jesus. They maintain, first, that it is difficult if not impossible to reconstruct the original setting and meaning of a parable and, second, that even when possible such an historical interpretation may leave the parable with little if anything to say to the present. Historical interpretation puts the parables at too great a distance from us. At issue, then, is whether to interpret the parables historically or in a more "relevant" way.

Dupont has put forward a suggestion which may resolve

this difficult issue. He insists, first, on the importance of historical analysis, observing that it alone ensures the objectivity which prevents our own arbitrary interpretations, or misinterpretations. He then goes on to observe that the experiences of the first hearers, to which the message of the parables is related, is not after all foreign to us; their experiences and ours are much the same, though lived in different historical situations. Thus we are not forced to make a choice between historical and contemporary interpretations; a sound interpretation will be both at once.

To illustrate the importance of objective, historical interpretation, it would be well to mention here two examples of parables interpreted without regard to the intention of Jesus. The first is cited by Dupont. In the Middle Ages, Catholic theologians interpreted the parable of the Weeds and the Wheat (Mt 13:24–30, 36–43) as a justification for burning heretics. We have here an example of *eis*egesis, the error of reading *into*, rather than lifting the proper meaning *out of*, the text, as responsible *ex*egesis does. These churchmen had *already* decided that they ought to burn heretics, before they went in search of a text to prove they were right (this is called "proof-texting"), then distorted the text to fit their preconception. The interpretation of the parable according to the intention of Jesus is quite the opposite of this. The parable exhorts us to patience. It teaches that we must allow the righteous and the wicked to co-exist until the end-time, for, like weeds and wheat, they look so alike that we cannot attempt to separate them without risking terrible errors. We must leave to God the role of separating the good and the evil at the final judgement.

The second example is the exemplary story of the Good Samaritan (Lk 10:29–37) which even today is sometimes interpreted as follows: The wounded man stands for humanity; the priest and Levite represent Judaism, which fails to have compassion; and the Samaritan stands for Jesus Christ, who alone heals and saves. Such an interpretation only evades the real meaning of the parable, that the deed of love, and not merely external religion, is what God requires of us—a hard lesson to hear, perhaps, but a supremely important one.

The most important of all guidelines for interpretation is that a parable be understood in accordance with Jesus' intention (as far as that can be determined). Otherwise we shall fail to hear the word of God. Rather than *hear* the message of the parables, we shall only be imposing upon them our own pet ideas. Once the original meaning of a parable is determined as nearly as possible, however, we must then go on to apply it to our own situation.

To summarize this chapter: A parable has three main settings: (a) its original context in Jesus' ministry; (b) its setting in the Gospel; and (c) its place in our own lives. Usually the exercise of interpretation involves getting behind the Gospel and back to the original meaning of the parable in the preaching of Jesus, then allowing the parable to speak to our own situation.

The guidelines for such interpretation are as follows: (1) We should seek to understand the meaning of the parable as a whole—its point or lesson—and its constituent meanings as well. While the parable as a whole is always tropical, its constituent meanings may or may not be tropes; the parts are to be interpreted in the context of the whole. "Allegorizing," the adding of tropes where there are none, is best avoided. (2) We should seek to arrive at the specific meaning of the original parable, and not just at a generalizing interpretation. (3) The parable should be interpreted historically, that is, in accordance with the intention of Jesus; otherwise, we are not truly hearing the word of God. Its application to our own Christian existence may then be explicitly drawn.

6. THE COMING OF GOD'S REIGN

A. The Reign of God

JEWS AND CHRISTIANS have always believed in a God who acts in history on behalf of his people. The Israelites often commemorated God's redemptive acts in the past, perhaps the greatest of which was the Exodus event, the liberation of their people from bondage in Egypt. The Israelites looked not only back but also forward. They hoped for a new and greater Exodus in the future. They longed for that day when God would definitely establish his reign over Israel and over all creation. Then God would destroy the evil powers, redeem his people, put down the mighty and exalt the lowly (Lk 1:52). He would inaugurate a new era of justice and peace. It is this saving activity of God in history which we call "the reign of God."

The word which I translate throughout this book as "reign" is, in the New Testament, the Greek word *basileia*. This in turn is a translation of the Aramaic word *malkuth*, the word which Jesus himself must have used. *Basileia* is an ambiguous word which can be translated either "reign" or "kingdom." *Malkuth*, however, is most accurately translated "reign." The word "kingdom" suggests a territory or a community. But the idea is rather of God reigning in our lives as individuals and as a society; it is *God's saving activity in history.* The reference is to God, his prevenient love for his people, his gracious acts on their behalf.

The expression "the reign of God," however, should not be understood as referring to God alone; it refers also to his people. It is a reality which transforms the existence of all humankind. If we should inquire as to what God's reign means for those who receive it, we would find no better answer than the one given in Jesus' sermon in the Nazareth synagogue (Lk 4:16–30). There, during the sabbath worship, Jesus opens the book of the prophet Isaiah and reads the following words:

> 18"The Spirit of the Lord is upon me, because he has anointed me to preach good news to the poor. He has sent me to proclaim release to the captives and recovering of sight to the blind, to set at liberty those who are oppressed, 19to proclaim the acceptable year of the Lord."
>
> (Lk 4:18–19; citation of Isa 61:1–2)

In the Year of Jubilee which Jesus here proclaims, not only are debts forgiven but a whole new social order is inaugurated. The reign of God, then, is liberation from all specific kinds of need and oppression. It is good news for "the poor," whom the Bible understands as the marginalized, that is, all those who stand helpless before the social, political, and religious power-structures.

An equivalent expression, which renders well the meaning of God's reign, and which clearly refers to both its religious and its social dimensions, to both God and humanity, is the "New Creation." This is the term which Paul employs in 2 Cor 5:16–21 to speak of the new humanity now reconciled to God through Christ (cf. Gal 6:15; Rom 8:21).

What is new and astonishing about the preaching of Jesus is that he proclaimed that God's reign was *now present*. At this very moment, he announced, it is entering into history: "The time is fulfilled, and the kingdom of God is at hand; repent, and believe in the gospel" (Mk 1:15; cf. Mt 4:17). This message is the ground of Jesus' ministry. All of his words and his works are properly understood only in reference to the breaking in of God's reign. His preaching and his actions, which confirm and illustrate each other, express his one mission as agent ushering in the reign of God.

By his temptation and his exorcisms, Jesus was beginning to win the final victory over the evil powers: "But if it is by the finger of God that I cast out demons, then the kingdom of God has come upon you" (Lk 11:20; cf. Mt 12:28). In the healing miracles and the preaching he bestowed the blessings of God's reign. When John the Baptist sent his disciples to ask, "Are you he who is to come, or shall we look for another?" Jesus replied: "Go and tell John what you have seen and heard: the blind receive their sight, the lame walk, lepers are cleansed, and the deaf hear, the dead are raised up, the poor have the good news preached to them" (Lk 7:18–23, which points back to 4:18–19; cf. Mt 11:2–6). Jesus demonstrated by sharing table fellowship with sinners that he brought to them the gift of God's forgiveness: "And as he sat at table in his house, many tax collectors and sinners were sitting with Jesus and his disciples" (Mk 2:15; Lk 15:1); he was sharply criticized for conducting himself in this way, for "the Pharisees and the scribes murmured, saying, 'This man receives sinners and eats with them'" (Lk 15:2; cf. Mk 2:16).

If God's reign is breaking into history, however, it has not yet come in power and glory (see Mk 9:1). God, at a time appointed by him, will definitively establish his reign over all creation. On that day of the Lord, the resurrection of the dead and the final judgment will take place, and the present era will give way to a new era without sin, suffering, or death. God's reign, then, is also to come *in the future*.

Thus, the reign of God is both present and future, both

"already and not yet." It is dynamic act or event. It is in this in-between time that Christians live out their existence in Christ Jesus.

The term used to speak of the ideas described here is "eschatology." The root of this word is the Greek noun *eschaton*, which means "the end." Eschatology is teaching about the last things, the end of the world or of history (as christology is teaching about Christ, ecclesiology about the Church, and so on).

It should be made clear at this point that the reign of God and the Church are not to be confounded. These are two distinct realities. The central reality in God's plan of salvation is his reign; to this the Church is subordinate. It is God's reign, and not the Church, that is the goal of all history. The Church serves as the sign and instrument of God's reign. Its role is to witness to the meaning and value of God's reign by its own life as a community. From this role derives the Church's mission of healing divisions and injustices of all kinds—the task of reconciliation in Christ. An historical example of such a ministry is Paul's apostleship to the Gentiles, his healing of the separation between Jew and Greek in the Church, a vocation which he understood as eschatological.

When Jesus proclaimed the coming of God's reign, his hearers must have pondered many things. When would it come? How? What would be its nature? Jesus' ministry was disconcerting; marked by reversals and failures, it hardly fulfilled the expectations for a reign of power and glory. Could this humble, inauspicious ministry be the beginning of God's reign? Since the Messiah was expected to separate the holy from the evil-doers to form a pure community, why did Jesus instead gather around himself sinners and tax-collectors? To questions such as these, Jesus replied in the parables we shall consider in this chapter.

These parables tell us much about Jesus himself, about his own understanding of his ministry and its relation to the coming of God's reign. Thus we can learn much christology from these parables. We do not have here a direct christology: Jesus does not apply titles to himself (such as Messiah or King of Israel) or make explicit claims about his identity and mission. Indirectly, however, he reveals much in these parables about his role as agent ushering in the reign of God.

B. The Growing Seed; the Mustard Seed; the Leaven

In the Gospel of Mark the similitudes of the Growing Seed and the Mustard Seed appear as a pair (Mk 4:26–29 and 30–32). In the Gospels of Matthew and Luke it is the similitudes of the Mustard Seed and the Leaven that are paired (Mt 13:31–32 and 33; Lk 13:18–19 and 20–21). The Growing Seed does not appear in Matthew or Luke; neither does the Leaven appear in Mark.

It is possible that these similitudes were uttered separately by Jesus and paired later by the primitive Church or the evangelists. While we find several paired parables in the Synoptic tradition, the pairs are not always constant. This means that the pairing may be secondary, and that in interpreting a parable we must not be overly influenced by a parable adjacent to it in the Gospel.

Whether originally spoken at the same time or separately, however, these three similitudes should be considered together. All three have to do with the coming of God's reign. They are preserved in one or both of our earliest sources (Q and Mark), a fairly strong attestation, so that we may be confident that Jesus did use parables to speak of the reign of God. Of that much we are certain; but beyond that, these similitudes, especially the Growing Seed, are not easy to interpret. What precisely they say about God's reign is not as clear as we might wish.

A much debated question has been whether these are similitudes of *growth* or of *contrast*: do they have to do with the gradual development of God's reign over a period of time, or with the sharp contrast between its insignificant beginning and splendid end? How one interprets them depends on one's understanding of the reign of God.

The "classical" interpretation of the nineteenth century was influenced by the evolutionary thought of the time. It understood the reign of God as a divine principle immanent in the world which develops until society is totally transformed in accordance with God's will. It thus interpreted these as similitudes of growth. This view did not give sufficient attention to the final, definitive coming of God's reign in the future. It is no longer widely held by biblical scholars. The reign of God is understood, not as an immanent evolution, but as God's gracious activity. God's reign does not grow; neither is it brought about by human effort.

The classical interpretation was replaced early in the twentieth century by the view called "thoroughgoing eschatology." According to this view, Jesus' preaching emphasized the coming of God's reign in the very near future. The point of these similitudes lies only in the final stage, which represents the sudden, catastrophic coming of God's reign. This interpretation, however, has the weakness of ignoring the middle stage, that of growth, depicted especially in the Growing Seed (Mk 4:26–29, especially vv. 27b–28).

A third view, advanced by C.H. Dodd, is called "realized eschatology." On this view, the final stage in these similitudes corresponds to the ministry of Jesus. That is, God's reign has already come, fully and definitively, in Jesus' ministry. These are similitudes of growth, but the growth corresponds to the history of Israel and the work of John the Baptist. The reign of God has come.

A widely held view, represented by Jeremias, attempts to do justice to both the present and the future. It speaks of "eschatology in the process of realization." Jeremias interprets these as similitudes of contrast, namely between insignificant beginning and triumphal end. But the end is implicit in the beginning; the event is already in process. The point of the similitudes is the assurance that God's hour is approaching. Nils A. Dahl has further refined this interpretation in an important article, "The Parables of Growth" (*Studia Theologica* 5 [1952] 132–66). Dahl does justice, not only to present and future, but to growth and contrast. In these similitudes, the initial stage stands for the unpropitious beginning of God's reign in the ministry of Jesus, the growth stands for the passage of time in history, and the final stage represents the coming of God's reign in power. The interpretation of Jeremias and Dahl seems to be the soundest, since it takes into account all aspects of Jesus' teaching about God's reign reflected in the Gospels. It is the view adopted in this book.

God's reign is thus both "already and not yet." The contrast is between small beginning and great end. The middle stage represents, not growth, but human history. History, controlled by God alone, follows a course predetermined by him. The final stage cannot come until all that God has ordained has happened.

Many must have pondered the question which the disciples of John the Baptist posed: "Are you he who is to come, or shall we look for another?" (Mt 11:3; Lk 7:19). The following three similitudes are a reply to the question whether the reign of God is now breaking in, and whether Jesus is the one to come.

THE GROWING SEED

Mk 4:26–29

[26]And he said,
"The kingdom of
God is as if a man
should scatter seed
upon the ground,
[27]and should sleep
and rise night and
day, and the seed
should sprout and
grow, he knows not
how. [28]The earth
produces of itself,
first the blade, then
the ear, then the full
grain in the ear.
[29]But when the
grain is ripe, at once
he puts in the sickle,
because the harvest
has come."

THE MUSTARD SEED

Mt 13:31–32	Mk 4:30–32	Lk 13:18–19
[31]Another parable he put before them, saying, "The kingdom of heaven	[30]And he said, "With what can we compare the kingdom of God, or what parable shall we use for it? [31]It	[18]He said therefore, "What is the kingdom of God like? And to what shall I compare it?
is like a grain of mustard seed which	is like a grain of mustard seed, which,	[19]It is like a grain of mustard seed which

a man took and sowed in his field; [32]it is the smallest of all seeds, but when it	when sown upon the ground, is the smallest of all the seeds on earth; [32]yet when it is sown it	a man took and sowed in his garden;
has grown it is the greatest of shrubs and becomes a tree,	grows up and becomes the greatest of all shrubs, and puts forth large branches,	and it grew and became a tree,
so that the birds of the air come and make nests in its branches."	so that the birds of the air can make nests in its shade."	and the birds of the air made nests in its branches."

THE LEAVEN

Mt 13:33		Lk 13:20–21
[33]He told them another parable. "The kingdom of heaven is like leaven which a woman took and hid in three measures of meal, till it was all leavened."		[20]And again he said, "To what shall I compare the kingdom of God? [21]It is like leaven which a woman took and hid in three measures of meal, till it was all leavened."

THE GROWING SEED

The similitude of the Growing Seed is special to Mark's Gospel. There it is paired with the similitude of the Mustard Seed. There are no indications that Mark made changes in the parable which he received from the tradition; he evidently incorporated it as he found it. The similitude has the marks of having originated in an

Aramaic-speaking environment. For example, in the East the day begins in the evening, so that a person first sleeps and then rises. Moreover, some phrases can be traced back to an Aramaic original. There is, then, no reason to doubt the essential authenticity of this similitude.

The Growing Seed is one of the most difficult of the Synoptic parables to interpret. Though its basic subject, the reign of God, is explicitly stated, and though the similitude is short and simple, its point is elusive. Dupont has summarized the main possible emphases: (a) the stress may be on the seed, or on the sower, or on both; (b) if on the seed, the point may be either its growth or the certainty of the harvest; (c) if on the sower, the point may be either his inactivity during the growth or his activity at the harvest.

What, then, did the similitude mean on Jesus' lips? The detail with which the growth of the seed is described, especially in vv. 27b–28, indicates that the center of the similitude is not the sower, but the seed—its sowing, growth, and harvest. But what happens to the seed must be viewed against the background of the sower's inactivity. The seed's ripening is independent of the sower's effort (as he goes about his daily routine it grows "of itself"). It is also mysterious ("he knows not how"). Finally, it is irresistible; the harvest will certainly come when the time is fulfilled, and it can neither be hurried along nor delayed. The similitude concludes with an indirect quotation of Joel 3:13a: "Put in the sickle, for the harvest is ripe." The harvest and sickle are a traditional biblical metaphor for the end of history and the judgment (cf. 4 Ezra [2 Esdras] 4:28–29, 35–39; Rev 14:15–16). This scriptural allusion provides the metaphor from which the similitude has been composed.

The similitude proclaims the coming of the reign of God, but it also says more. Its point is not only the fact *that* the reign of God will come, for of that the Jewish audience of Jesus had no doubt; its lesson lies in *how* it comes. Before the harvest, the sowing and growth must take place; before the end of the world and the judgment, a certain process must take place in accordance with God's plan. It is God alone who, by a series of events, leads history to its goal.

Jesus' ministry, in which nothing seemed to be happening, looked very little like the beginning of God's reign. Some must have wondered why he did not engage in any active intervention of a political, nationalist sort, later engaged in by the Zealots. Jesus replies that he does not need to engage in any messianic activity. The eschatological process is taking place, independently, mysteriously, irresistibly, in his preaching and deeds. When the time is ripe, God will certainly intervene to establish his reign in power.

THE MUSTARD SEED

The Mustard Seed appears in all three Synoptic Gospels. It was preserved in two sources, Q and Mark. Luke incorporates the Q version in purer form, while Matthew as usual conflates (that is, combines) the Q and Markan versions. Since it is attested in both of our earliest sources, Q and Mark, this similitude is one of the instances of Jesus' teaching whose authenticity is most certain.

Both Q and Mark introduce the similitude with a double question; it has the Jewish poetic form of two parallel lines and is a typical rabbinic introduction to parables. The introduction gives the basic meaning of the similitude: it has to do with the reign of God. This introduction is preserved in both Q and Mark, the strongest possible attestation: we can therefore be certain that Jesus used similitudes such as this one to speak of God's reign. But God's reign is not here compared precisely to the mustard seed itself; rather, it is compared to the entire process, to all that happens to the mustard seed in this narrative.

The main features in the two versions are identical: the reign of God is compared to the small mustard seed which grows into a plant so large that it can provide shelter for the birds of the air. These common features belong to the earliest stage of the similitude we can recover and are therefore probably authentic. (The differences in the two verions are worth noting; they provide an interesting example of the modifications which a literary unit might undergo during the period of oral transmission and in the composition of the Gospels.)

A feature common to Q and Mark, and therefore probably an original part of the similitude, is the final description of the plant as great enough to provide shelter for birds. This image is taken from the Old Testament (Ezek 17:22–24; cf. 31:1–18; Dan 4:10–27). Ezekiel says of a noble cedar to be planted by God: "in the shade of its branches birds of every sort will nest" (Ezek 17:23). This biblical image is a metaphor for a mighty kingdom providing protection for its subject-states. It is owing to the influence of these scriptural passages that Q calls the mustard plant a "tree," and that both Q and Mark say the birds make "nests" in it. In other Jewish literature, birds are an eschatological metaphor for Gentiles seeking refuge with Israel.

With respect to botany, both Q and Mark are incorrect: the mustard seed is not the smallest of all seeds, though it may seem so to the farmer. Neither does it grow into a tree with great branches; it is a shrub, one of the largest herbs, growing in Israel to a height of six to ten feet. The birds alight on it, not to build nests, but to take shelter in the shade and to pluck the seeds.

Certainly the meaning of the similitude lies in the contrast between the smallness of the mustard seed and the greatness of the full-grown shrub, so large that the birds can find shelter in it. This interpretation is sometimes questioned on the grounds that the Q version does not mention the tiny size of the seed, and that this point is therefore not significant. We can be sure, however, that it is implied in Q, since the smallness of the mustard seed was proverbial in Israel, and would have come to the mind of any hearer; in the Synoptics, specifically in Q, Jesus speaks of "faith as a grain of mustard seed" which could move a mountain

(Mt 17:20; cf. Lk 17:6). The Markan version only makes explicit what is implicit in the Q version. Finally, the versions of both Q and Mark conclude by describing the impressive size of this shrub or, hyperbolically, this tree, in which the birds take shelter; this conclusion is no doubt intended as a contrast to the seed. The hyperbole shows what we have to do with the eschatological. This similitude, then, is clearly about the contrast between the small beginnings and the final greatness of God's reign.

The Jews expected the reign of God to be glorious and universal; little of this was evident in Jesus' ministry, which was small, beset by failure, unpromising. Yet it is precisely in such humble beginnings that God is now beginning to establish his reign, which will include Gentiles as well as Jews within its scope. Even a shrub as impressive as the mustard plant giving shelter to birds has its beginning in a tiny seed.

THE LEAVEN

We cannot be certain that the Leaven was originally spoken at the same time as the Mustard Seed, although both Matthew and Luke give evidence of their belonging together: Matthew speaks of the Leaven as "another parable" and Luke writes "again he said." The introduction, that the reign of God "is like leaven," does not mean that the comparison is to the leaven itself; rather it is to all that occurs when leaven is hidden in meal. In the Q version of the Mustard Seed the character is presumably a man; in the Leaven, it is a woman. The work of a man and a woman are equally worthy analogies for the coming of God's reign.

Leaven was a traditional metaphor for an evil thing having a great effect (see Mk 8:15; 1 Cor 5:6; Gal 5:9). Here Jesus boldly uses it in the opposite sense, as a metaphor for the coming of God's reign. The quantity of meal, "three measures" (perhaps taken from Gen 18:6), is enormous: it is approximately 50 pounds or 40 liters of flour, which would produce enough bread to feed a hundred people. This hyperbolic feature demonstrates that we are dealing with divine realities.

The meaning of the similitude lies in the effect which the hidden leaven has on the great batch of meal. The point is not only the power of the leaven, but also its hiddenness: the woman "hid" the leaven in the meal. A power presently at work is not always obvious. God's reign was expected to bring revolutionary change in the life of Israel and the world, but no such change could be seen in Jesus' ministry. Jesus says, in answer to such doubts, that neither can one initially see the effect of leaven which a woman hides in meal. By his very preaching and deeds, God's reign is already quietly at work.

Summary

In all three similitudes, we see the relation between the apparently insignificant ministry of Jesus and the coming of God's reign in power and glory. The wonderful message of these similitudes is that Jesus' ministry is related to the final coming of God's reign as the sowing and growth are related to the harvest, the seed to the shrub, the leaven to the loaves. Precisely through what seems insignificant God's reign comes. These similitudes, especially the two about seed, illustrate perfectly the paradox that the reign of God is at once present and future. Just as the full-grown harvest or shrub is in some way already contained in the seed, but does not yet exist, so God's reign is already breaking in with the words and works of Jesus, but has not yet fully come. In the Growing Seed, the aspect given special emphasis is the mysteriousness and certainty of the event which is now in process; in the Mustard Seed, it is the contrast between the small beginnings and the great end; and in the Leaven it is the hiddenness of the energy already at work. We are here given an exciting glimpse into Jesus' self-understanding.

C. The Sower

THE SOWER

Mt 13:3–9, 18–23	**Mk 4:3–9, 14–20**	**Lk 8:5–8, 11–15**
3 And he told them many things in parables, saying:	3 "Listen!	
A sower went out to sow. 4 And as	"A sower went out to sow. 4 And as	5 "A sower went out to sow his seed; and as he sowed,
he sowed, some seeds fell along the path,	he sowed, some seed fell along the path,	some fell along the path, and was trodden under foot,
and the birds came and devoured them.	and the birds came and devoured it.	and the birds of the air devoured it.
5 Other seeds fell on rocky ground, where they had not much soil, and immediately	5 Other seed fell on rocky ground, where it had not much soil, and immediately	6 And some fell on the rock;
they sprang up, since they had no depth of soil, 6 but when the sun rose they were scorched; and since they had no root they	it sprang up, since it had no depth of soil; 6 and when the sun rose it was scorched, and since it had no root it	and as it grew up,
withered away.	withered away.	it withered away, because it had no moisture.
7 Other seeds fell upon thorns, and the thorns grew up and choked them.	7 Other seed fell among thorns and the thorns grew up and choked it, and it yielded no grain.	7 And some fell among thorns; and the thorns grew with it and choked it.

8 Other seeds fell on good soil and brought forth grain,	8 And other seeds fell into good soil and brought forth grain,	8 And some fell into good soil
	growing up and increasing and	and grew,
some a hundredfold, some sixty, some thirty.	yielding thirtyfold and sixtyfold and a hundredfold."	and yielded a hundredfold."
	9 And he said,	As he said this, he called out,
9 He who has ears, let him hear."	"He who has ears, to hear, let him hear."	"He who has ears to hear, let him hear."
18 "Hear then the parable of the sower.		11 "Now the parable is this:
	14 The sower sows the word.	The seed is the word of God.
19 When any one hears the word of the kingdom and does not understand it,	15 And these are the ones along the path, where the word is sown; when they	12 The ones along the path are those who have heard; then the
the evil one comes and snatches away what is sown in his heart; this is what was sown along the path.	hear, Satan immediately comes and takes away the word which is sown in them.	devil comes and takes away the word from their hearts, that they may not believe and be saved.
20 As for what was sown on rocky ground, this is he who hears the word and immediately receives it with joy;	16 And these in like manner are the ones sown upon rocky ground, who, when they hear the word, immediately receive it with joy;	13 And the ones on the rock are those who, when they hear the word receive it with joy;
21 yet he has no root in himself, but endures for a while, and when tribulation or persecution arises	17 and they have no root in themselves, but endure for a while; then when tribulation or persecution arises	but these have no root, they believe for a while and in time of temptation

on account of the word, immediately he falls away.	on account of the word, immediately they fall away.	fall away.
22 As for what was sown among thorns, this is he who hears the word,	18 And others are the ones sown among thorns; they are those who hear the word,	14 And as for what fell among the thorns, they are those who hear,
but the cares of the world and the delight in riches	19 but the cares of the world, and the delight in riches, and the desire for other things, enter in and	but as they go on their way they are choked by the cares and riches and pleasures of life, and their
choke the word, and it proves unfruitful.	choke the word, and it proves unfruitful.	fruit does not mature.
23 As for what was sown on good soil, this is he who hears the word and understands it; he indeed bears fruit, and yields, in one case a hundredfold, in another sixty, and in another thirty."	20 But those that were sown upon the good soil are the ones who hear the word and accept it and bear fruit, thirtyfold and sixtyfold and a hundredfold."	15 And as for that in the good soil, they are those who, hearing the word, hold it fast in an honest and good heart, and bring forth fruit with patience."

The parable of the Sower appears in Chapter 4 of Mark's Gospel with the similitudes of the Growing Seed and the Mustard Seed. Because all three employ the image of seed, and because they appear together, exegetes usually interpret the parable in light of the similitudes, taking it as a variation on the same theme. Caution is called for, however. These parables were not necessarily uttered by Jesus on the same occasion, and so the Sower should be interpreted on its own terms. The task is by no means easy, however; it is exceedingly difficult, if not impossible, to ascertain the original meaning of this parable.

Few scholars have doubted the authenticity of the parable itself. The method of sowing accurately reflects the custom in Israel. There sowing precedes plowing; the sower intended to plow up the temporary path and the stubble after sowing. He was thus not as careless as it would seem. The language, too, shows traces of an Aramaic original.

The majority of exegetes believe, however, that the interpretation appended to the parable in Mark's Gospel (and taken over by Matthew and Luke) is secondary and incorrect. It is pointed out that the Markan interpretation is one of only three interpretations in the Synoptic Gospels which is a detailed, point-by-point explanation of the parable; the other two, appended to the Weeds and the Wheat and to the Fishnet, are both peculiar to Matthew and both secondary. The Markan interpretation is said to shift the meaning of the parable from the eschatological to the psychological and exhortative. Moreover, the trials and tribulations depicted in the interpretation are thought to presuppose the period of the Church, when there had been sufficient time for apostasy and for persecution.

The most widely held interpretation is that, in the parable itself, the seed falling on the first three types of soil, which fail to bear fruit, all stand for one thing: apparent obstacles and reversals in Jesus' ministry. In contrast, the seed falling on the fourth and last type of soil, which bears much fruit, represents final, certain success. Perhaps the most striking feature of the parable is the abundance of the harvest. A tenfold yield was considered good, so that the thirty-, sixty-, and hundredfold yield is extraordinarily abundant. This represents the eschatological overflowing of divine blessings. The lesson of the parable is that, despite what seem to be frustrations and failures in Jesus' ministry, it will certainly bear fruit, and in a manner exceeding all expectations. The parable was addressed to those who wondered whether the words and deeds of Jesus could be linked to the reign of God; it is an encouragement to those with little faith or hope. The parable would thus have been another answer to the question whether Jesus could be the coming one.

A minority of interpreters, however, think that the Markan interpretation may render the original meaning of the parable. The parable is thus a lesson on hearing and doing the word. The Markan interpretation is, to be sure, more detailed and elaborate than those of most Synoptic parables. It is quite possible, however, that Jesus originally drew a simple contrast between those who failed and those who succeeded in receiving and keeping the word, and that later the evangelist (or a predecessor), following the main line of thought, embroidered further details. If the Markan interpretation is original, at least in its main point, then the background of the expression "the word" is the prophetic literature of the Old Testament. An interesting example occurs in Isa 55:10–11, where God's word is compared to rain and snow which make the earth "bring forth and sprout." (A parallel to this parable appears in 4 Ezra [2 Esdras] 9:31–37 where the seed sown in humanity is the law. Cf. 4 Ezra 4:28–32; 8:41–45.)

D. The Weeds and the Wheat; the Fishnet

Some of those who observed Jesus must have wondered why, if God's reign was breaking in, he did not endeavor to separate the righteous from sinners and to establish a pure and holy messianic community. We know that other groups in Israel aspired to such an ideal. The Pharisees, whose name means "separated ones," understood themselves as a holy community strictly observing the law. So did the Essenes, the sectarian "community of the new covenant" which produced the Dead Sea Scrolls. John the Baptist's activity, too, was directed to gathering a holy community; he spoke of the Messiah as one who would separate the wheat and the chaff (Mt 3:12; Lk 3:17). Jesus rejected this way of acting. His disciples included persons of all types: not only those generally regarded as righteous, but also the simple people of the land (considered ignorant of the law by the Pharisees), tax collectors and sinners, and the like. Jesus must have aroused wonder and indignation for gathering such a mixed community. He responded to the question, or reproach, in the parable of the Weeds and the Wheat and the similitude of the Fishnet. It is unlikely that these two parables were spoken at the same time, but they are closely related in meaning. In these parables, Jesus said that he would call all persons without distinction; there remained time for repentance; he would leave to God the work of separating the righteous and the wicked at the hour appointed by him. Both parables are eschatological; they have to do with the final judgment, which they compare to a separation.

THE WEEDS AND THE WHEAT

Mt 13:24–30, 36–43

24Another parable he put before them, saying, "The kingdom of heaven may be compared to a man who sowed good seed in his field; 25but while men were sleeping, his enemy came and sowed weeds among the wheat, and went away. 26So when the plants came up and bore grain, then the weeds appeared also. 27And the servants of the householder came and said to him, 'Sir, did you not sow good seed in your field? How then has it weeds?' 28He said to them, 'An enemy has done this.' The servants said to him, 'Then do you want us to go and gather them?' 29But he said, 'No; lest in gathering the weeds you root up the wheat along with them. 30Let both grow together until the harvest; and at harvest time I will tell the reapers, Gather the weeds first and bind them in bundles to be burned, but gather the wheat into my barn.'"

36Then he left the crowds and went into the house. And his disciples came to him, saying "Explain to us the parable of the weeds of the field." [37]He answered, "He who sows the good seed is the Son of man; [38]the field is the world, and the good seed means the sons of the kingdom; the weeds are the sons of the evil one, [39]and the enemy who sowed them is the devil; the harvest is the close of the age, and the reapers are angels. [40]Just as the weeds are gathered and burned with fire, so will it be at the close of the age. [41]The Son of man will send his angels, and they will gather out of his kingdom all causes of sin and all evildoers, [42]and throw them into the furnace of fire; there men will weep and gnash their teeth. [43]Then the righteous will shine like the sun in the kingdom of their Father. He who has ears, let him hear."

THE FISHNET

Mt 13:47–50

[47]"Again, the kingdom of heaven is like a net which was thrown into the sea and gathered fish of every kind; [48]when it was full, men drew it ashore and sat down and sorted the good into vessels but threw away the bad. [49]So it will be at the close of the age. The angels will come out and separate the evil from the righteous, [50]and throw them into the furnace of fire; there men will weep and gnash their teeth."

THE WEEDS AND THE WHEAT

A few interpreters have suggested that this parable, which is peculiar to Matthew, is his revision of the similitude of the Growing Seed, which neither he nor Luke took over from Mark. Most exegetes, however, think this unlikely; the parable of the Weeds and the Wheat stands on its own.

The parable begins, "The kingdom of heaven [Matthew's

preferred expression] may be compared to a man" (v. 24); the comparison, however, is not to the man, but to all that is narrated about the weeds and the wheat.

A few explanatory observations on the narrative: The first half of the parable (vv. 24–28a) serves only to show that the owner is not responsible for the appearance of the weeds. The center of the parable is the problem addressed by the servants' question, whether they should tear up the weeds (v. 28b); the point of the parable lies in the second half (vv. 28b–30). The type of weed, darnel, closely resembles wheat in the early stage of growth. It would be normal to pull up the weeds, and the servants' question is appropriate, but evidently the weeds have become widespread, and their roots may have become intertwined with those of the wheat—hence the master's directive that they be allowed to grow together until the harvest. The weeds would be gathered in bundles to be burned as fuel, which was scarce in Israel.

The weeds and the wheat are, of course, metaphors for wicked and righteous persons; the harvest, as mentioned earlier, was a traditional metaphor for the end of history, and fire was a traditional metaphor for punishment.

Very likely the servants' question (v. 28b) represents the view of some among Jesus' hearers, and the owner's reply (vv. 29–30) represents the view of Jesus. The parable is an exhortation to patience. In this parable Jesus explicitly rejects the suggestion that the good and the bad be prematurely separated in his ministry. For one thing, these may look so alike (as do weeds and wheat) that any attempt to separate them would involve the risk of terrible errors. Besides, the time for separation has not yet come; there is still the opportunity for repentance. Jesus teaches that he and his disciples must allow the good and the wicked to co-exist, and leave to God the role of separating them at the time appointed by him alone. Jesus will not, in his ministry, anticipate the work of God.

Exegetes are generally of the opinion that the interpretation appended to the parable (vv. 36–43), given in private to the disciples, is a secondary addition made by Matthew himself. The evangelist may have composed it on the model of the private interpretation of the Sower, which he took over from Mark. The application is in two parts: vv. 37–39 consist of a point-by-point interpretation of seven elements in the parable, and vv. 40–43 have to do with the fate of the evil-doers and the righteous at the final judgment. The interpretation is overly detailed. Even if added secondarily by the evangelist, however, the interpretation is basically an accurate rendering of the parable's meaning. A shift in emphasis is, nevertheless, evident. The community which the evangelist now has in mind is the Church, the kingdom of the Son of man. Moreover, the interpretation stresses, not the need for patience (the original point) but the threat of the final judgment; members of the Christian community are warned that there will be a separation of the holy and the evil in the judgment to come.

THE FISHNET

We cannot know with certainty whether the similitude of the Fishnet (not necessarily spoken by Jesus in private, as v. 36 suggests), was addressed to the crowd, or to Jesus' disciples, those whom he called "fishers of men" (Mk 1:17; cf. Mt 4:19; Lk 5:10). Again we have the introduction, "the kingdom of Heaven is like a net"; but the comparison is not to the net only but to all that occurs with respect to the catch of fish and their sorting out (vv. 47–48).

The type of net used for fishing in the Sea of Galilee (also called Lake Gennesaret) is a seine-net which is drawn through the water either between two boats or from one boat to the shore. This net catches fish "of every kind," that is, both edible and inedible. (See Lev 11:9–12 for the laws on clean and unclean fish.) The latter are thrown away (not back into the water).

This parable, too, has to do with separation. Jesus had

said to his disciples, "I will make you fishers of men"; the metaphor provides the basis for this similitude. The fisher cannot be selective with respect to the fish to be caught by the net; the sorting out can take place only afterward. Likewise the appeal of Jesus and his disciples must go out to all. Jesus' ministry was to all persons and groups without discrimination. Jesus will not prejudge. Only when the time is fulfilled ("when it was full," v. 48), will God, at the final judgment, separate the righteous and the wicked.

The appended interpretation (vv. 49–50) is clearly the redactional work of the evangelist Matthew. A close reading shows that this interpretation replicates the interpretation of the Weeds and the Wheat (vv. 40b–43). The evangelist has made two slips: to say that those who separate will "come out" (v. 49) applies to reapers but not to fishers, and throwing "into the furnace of fire" (v. 50) applies to weeds but not to fish. Nevertheless, the evangelist has accurately rendered the essential meaning of the similitude.

7. THE GRACE OF GOD'S REIGN

A. *Jesus, The Righteous, and Sinners*

JESUS ANNOUNCED the coming of God's reign not only by his preaching but also by his actions. One of the characteristic works of Jesus' ministry was his association with religious outcasts. Jesus shared table fellowship with those referred to in the Gospels as "tax collectors and sinners"; he not only ate in their homes, but he received them as well, acting as their host at table. For this revolutionary behavior, Jesus was sharply criticized by the religious elite, those whom the Gospels refer to as "the scribes and the Pharisees." Being religiously exclusive, they shunned the impure, and regarded Jesus' actions as irreligious.

Jesus' aim in the parables considered in this chapter was to justify his preaching of the good news to the poor. It is because God is infinitely loving, and rejoices greatly over the sinner who repents, that Jesus shares table companionship with the outcast and the despised. The sinners' drawing near to him is an expression of their repentance; his receiving them at table is a sign of God's forgiveness (see Lk 15:1–2). The outpouring of God's forgiveness on repentant sinners is one of the signs of the coming of God's reign.

These parables, then, and their settings and interpretations, cast people into two very different groups. Those in one group are called "tax collectors and sinners"; they represent all religious outcasts. This group included those who were openly immoral (e.g., thieves, adulterers); it also included those who held occupations involving dishonesty, such as tax collectors and shepherds (given to fraud, embezzlement, and the like) and who were therefore stripped of such civil rights as holding office and testifying in court. Those in the other group are called "the scribes and the Pharisees"; they stand for all the self-righteous. It is important to note that Jesus shared table fellowship equally with persons of both groups.

The parables discussed in this chapter have three main points: they portray God's boundless love and mercy; they justify Jesus' mission to sinners; and they rebuke Jesus' critics who cannot understand or affirm God's love for all.

One of the most significant elements of these parables is their implicit christology. Jesus understands that in his association with sinners he is acting on God's behalf. It is in Jesus' table fellowship with sinners that God's forgiveness of them is actualized. The parables thus make an indirect claim to authority: Jesus claims to be acting as God's representative. We are again given an important insight into Jesus' self-understanding.

B. The Laborers in the Vineyard

THE LABORERS IN THE VINEYARD

Mt 20:1–16

1 "For the kingdom of heaven is like a householder who went out early in the morning to hire laborers for his vineyard. 2 After agreeing with the laborers for a denarius a day, he sent them into his vineyard. 3 And going out about the third hour he saw others standing idle in the market place; 4 and to them he said, 'You go into the vineyard too, and whatever is right I will give you.' So they went.

> [5]Going out again about the sixth hour and the ninth hour, he did the same. [6]And about the eleventh hour he went out and found others standing; and he said to them, 'Why do you stand here idle all day?' [7]They said to him, 'Because no one has hired us.' He said to them, 'You go into the vineyard too.' [8]And when evening came, the owner of the vineyard said to his steward, 'Call the laborers and pay them their wages, beginning with the last, up to the first.' [9]And when those hired about the eleventh hour came, each of them received a denarius. [10]Now when the first came, they thought they would receive more; but each of them also received a denarius. [11]And on receiving it they grumbled at the householder, [12]saying, 'These last worked only one hour, and you have made them equal to us who have borne the burden of the day and scorching heat.' [13]But he replied to one of them, 'Friend, I am doing you no wrong; did you not agree with me for a denarius? [14]Take what belongs to you, and go; I choose to give to this last as I give to you. [15]Am I not allowed to do what I choose with what belongs to me? Or do you begrudge my generosity?' [16]So the last will be first, and the first last."

This is one of the most striking of the parables in which Jesus vindicates the good news to the poor. This parable illustrates, in quite an arresting way, the grace of God's reign. In it Jesus shows that God's reign does not follow the *quid pro quo* rules of recompense; it is, instead, spontaneous, unearned, overflowing gift. Jesus here invites his critics to leave their old view and to accept this new view of God's reign.

This parable, which appears in Matthew's Gospel alone, is there spoken to the disciples; that is most likely a secondary audience or setting. Jesus himself probably addresses the parable to scribes and Pharisees. We have here an example of a change in a parable's social context.

Though the parable begins, "the kingdom of God is like a householder," God's reign is here compared, not to a householder, but to a reckoning. The reckoning was a traditional Jewish metaphor for the coming of God's reign which Jesus took over and made his own.

The parable falls into two parts. The first part (vv. 1–8) narrates the householder's hiring of the laborers and his issuing of instructions for their payment. The employer hires groups of workers at five different times during the day, the first at dawn ("early in the morning," v. 1) and the last at the end of the afternoon ("the eleventh hour," around 5 p.m., v. 6). He agrees to give the first hired a denarius, the usual wage for a day's work, and the others "whatever is right" (vv. 2, 4). Those still unemployed at the end of the day are not guilty of indolence; no one has yet hired them (vv. 6–7). The workers are paid that evening (see Lev 19:13; Dt 24:14–15). They are paid "beginning with the last" (which may mean simply, "including the last") so that in the story "the first" can know how much they receive; there is no other significance to this detail (v. 8b). All are given the same amount, one denarius; this was a mere subsistence wage.

The second part (vv. 9–15) recounts the paying of the wages, the grumbling of the first hired, who by now had come to expect *more* than one denarius, and the response of the householder. The protesters feel their treatment doubly unfair; they have worked around 12 hours, the others only one; they have toiled in the midday heat, the others in the cool of dusk.

The stress lies on the second half of the parable. Its point is the householder's generosity to those hired at the eleventh hour. The eleventh-hour workers stand for the religious outcasts who were answering Jesus' call to God's reign. Those hired earlier, who grumbled that they deserved more, stand for the righteous, who protested that they merited special reward.

It is important to note that the workers employed first are not treated unjustly, though it may seem so: they receive the day's pay which they and the employer had agreed upon at the outset. Their complaint has to do with the fact that the workers employed last, though they had toiled only one hour, had received the same day's pay. The last hired have not earned a day's wage; it is given them out of the employer's generosity. "The first" cannot tolerate the fact that the recompense of "the last" is in large part an unearned gift. The protesters, who stand for the scribes and Pharisees, speak of merit; the householder, who stands for God, speaks of grace.

This parable compares God to a householder who has compassion on the poor, who knows that an hour's wage will not provide subsistence; he bestows upon the outcast and the despised the gifts of his reign. This, says Jesus, is how God acts; and it is because God acts in this way that I associate with sinners. There is no better interpretation of the parable than the concluding question of the householder: "do you begrudge my generosity?"—which literally in the Greek is, "are you envious because I am good?" (v. 15).

It would be well to dismiss a common but incorrect interpretation of this parable. The interpretation added by Matthew in v. 16 is secondary. This parable is not about the reversal of order on the last day. Matthew gives it that interpretation by placing it in the context of Peter's question about rewards on the last day and Jesus' saying about reversal (19:27, 30; cf. Mk 9:35; 10:31; Lk 13:30). But this misrenders the parable's meaning. The detail of the reversal of the workers when they are paid (v. 8b), as noted above, does not have the significance which Matthew's concluding verse (v. 16) gives to it.

C. The Two Sons; the Two Debtors; the Pharisee and the Tax Collector

THE TWO SONS

Mt 21:28–32

28 "What do you think? A man had two sons; and he went to the first and said, 'Son, go and work in the vine-

> yard today.' [29]And he answered, 'I will not'; but afterward he repented and went. [30]And he went to the second and said the same; and he answered, 'I go, sir,' but did not go. [31]Which of the two did the will of his father?" They said, "The first." Jesus said to them, "Truly, I say to you, the tax collectors and the harlots go into the kingdom of God before you. [32]For John came to you in the way of righteousness, and you did not believe him, but the tax collectors and the harlots believed him; and even when you saw it, you did not afterward repent and believe him."

This parable is peculiar to Matthew's Gospel. Though it is brief, it responds perhaps more pointedly than any other parable to the critics who objected to Jesus' association with sinners.

The first son stands for the tax collectors and the harlots (v. 31). The second son stands for the chief priests, the elders, and the Pharisees (vv. 23, 45). This is a two-edged parable. It is a vindication of the preaching of the good news to the poor; they repent and respond to God's call. It is also a stern rebuke to the complacent; elsewhere in Matthew Jesus says of the scribes and Pharisees, "they preach, but do not practice" (Mt 23:3).

The parable functions much like Nathan's parable of the Ewe Lamb addressed to David (2 Sam 12:1–7; quoted above in Chapter 1): the hearers (the chief priests, elders, and Pharisees), invited to pass judgment on the characters in the story, are drawn into convicting themselves. From their own lips comes the verdict: it is the first son who did his parent's will. The original ending of the parable is the saying addressed to these critics: "Truly, I say to you, the tax collectors and the harlots go into the kingdom of God before you" (v. 31). In several instances the formula, "truly, I say to you," marks the conclusion of a parable.

The application to the Baptist (v. 32) is not an original part of the parable. It occurs as an independent unit in Lk 7:29–30. It probably came to Matthew together with the parable, having been appended to it during the period of oral transmission.

THE TWO DEBTORS

Lk 7:41–43

> [41]"A certain creditor had two debtors; one owed five hundred denarii, and the other fifty. [42]When they could not pay, he forgave them both. Now which of them will love him more?" [43]Simon answered, "The one, I suppose, to whom he forgave more." And he said to him, "You have judged rightly."

This parable, preserved in Luke alone, is much like that of the Two Sons: it has two characters, who stand for repentant sinners and the self-righteous respectively. It, too, is a two-edged parable, justifying the good news to the poor and rebuking the officially religious.

In Luke's Gospel, this parable occurs in the context of the story of the woman, a sinner, who weeps at Jesus' feet, wipes them with her hair, and anoints them with ointment in the house of Simon the Pharisee (Lk 7:36–50). Simon, who can see in her only a sinner, wonders how Jesus could allow this woman to touch him. Jesus answers by telling the short but profound parable of the Two Debtors. It contrasts a great debt and deep gratitude with a small debt and slight gratitude. Again, it is the hearer himself, Simon, who pronounces judgment: surely the one to whom more is forgiven is the one who loves more, that is, who feels the deepest thankfulness. Thus does Simon convict himself. It is out of the depth of poverty that one understands the depth of God's goodness. The beautiful story of the woman who anoints Jesus' feet comes to a close when Jesus says to her: "Your faith has saved you; go in peace" (v. 50). The lesson of the Two Sons and the Two Debtors is the same: it is repentant sinners, and not the self-righteous, who are near to God.

THE PHARISEE AND THE TAX COLLECTOR

Lk 18:9–14

> [9]He also told this parable to some who trusted in themselves that they were righteous and despised others:
> [10]"Two men went up into the temple to pray, one a
> Pharisee and the other a tax collector. [11]The Pharisee
> stood and prayed thus with himself, 'God, I thank thee that I am not like other men, extortioners, unjust,
> adulterers, or even like this tax collector. [12]I fast twice a
> week, I give tithes of all that I get.' [13]But the tax collector,
> standing far off, would not even lift up his eyes to heaven, but beat his breast, saying, 'God, be merciful to me a sinner!' [14]I tell you, this man went down to his house justified rather than the other; for every one who exalts himself will be humbled, but he who humbles himself will be exalted."

For Jesus it is a spiritual law that the repentant sinner is nearer to God than the self-righteous. This exemplary story, as its introductory verse says, is addressed to the complacent, that is, to those who place their trust in themselves rather than in God. Both the language and the details of the story, recorded only in Luke's Gospel, indicate a Palestinian origin of this exemplary story. Again we have two contrasting characters, one of whom stands for the self-satisfied, the other for repentant sinners.

We are given a striking picture of two men praying in the temple: one, a Pharisee, standing with eyes and hands raised up toward heaven, the usual posture in prayer; the other, a tax collector, standing off at a distance, with eyes downcast and hand beating his breast.

In his prayer, the Pharisee lists first the sins from which he has refrained. He even compares himself favorably to the tax collector. He then lists his good deeds. Though the law required fasting only once a year, on the Day of Atonement, he voluntarily fasted twice a week, on Mondays and

Thursdays, perhaps as atonement for others' sins. He also gave tithes of all that he purchased, a pious work which involved self-denial. A prayer much like this one is preserved in the Babylonian Talmud; thus it is taken from real life. The Pharisee gives thanks to God, and asks for nothing; he knows that all he is he owes to God. His prayer is one of thanksgiving, not of petition.

Next we have the prayer of the tax collector. Tax collectors were held in very low esteem. They were generally considered to be as dishonest as robbers. They had no civil rights. As disreputable persons, they were generally avoided. The customs (though not other taxes) of each district were farmed out to the highest bidder among tax collectors. The amount of the customs was set by the state, but the tax collectors, who realized a profit out of the transaction, had their ways of defrauding people.

This tax collector prays, not daring even to raise his eyes; he beats his breast, that is, his heart, the seat of sin, as an expression of deep remorse. He can do nothing but cry out to God for mercy. He and his family are in a desperate situation. Amends would require not only the abandonment of his sinful livelihood, but restitution of all his dishonestly acquired gains plus an additional one-fifth.

Surely the conclusion, "this man went down to his house justified rather than the other" (v. 14) shocked the original hearers. The word "justified" means accepted by God, right with God. The exemplary story does not say that the tax collector was righteous and the Pharisee was not; quite the contrary. The Pharisee had done no wrong; in his prayer he had thanked God and asked for nothing. The tax collector had not yet taken any steps to make amends. The point is that it is precisely the contrite sinner whom God justifies. The tax collector's cry is reminiscent of the opening verse of Psalm 51: "Have mercy on me, O God." The psalmist goes on to say: "The sacrifice acceptable to God is a broken spirit; a broken and contrite heart, O God, thou wilt not despise" (v. 17). God receives those who in repentance implore his mercy rather than those who remind him of their supposed virtuous achievements. God acts in this way, Jesus says, and therefore so do I.

It is uncertain whether the saying in v. 14b was an original part of the exemplary story. It appears also at the end of the teaching on places at table in Luke (Lk 14:11; cf. Lk 1:52) and as an independent saying in Mt 23:12. Some interpreters object that it makes the exemplary story a general moral lesson on humility; others think it expresses well the meaning of the exemplary story.

D. The Lost Sheep; the Lost Coin; the Prodigal Son

In Luke's Gospel, the Lost Sheep and the Lost Coin are twin similitudes; they are followed immediately by the related parable of the Prodigal Son. All three are about the joy of finding what was lost. Of these three, only the Lost Sheep appears in Matthew's Gospel.

This chapter in Luke's Gospel (ch. 15) begins as follows: "Now the tax collectors and sinners were all drawing near to him. And the Pharisees and the scribes murmured, saying, 'This man receives sinners and eats with them'" (Lk 15:1–2). These groups of people symbolize all religious outcasts and all the self-righteous respectively. That Jesus acts as host at table for sinners is regarded as irreligious behavior. It is in response to this criticism that Jesus addresses these three parables to the Pharisees and scribes. In them, table fellowship alludes to the joy of the new age; it may also point to the celebration of the Lord's Supper.

THE LOST SHEEP AND THE LOST COIN

Mt 18:12–14	**Lk 15:3–7, 8–10**
12 "What do you think? If a man has a hundred	3 So he told them this parable: 4 "What man of you, having a hundred

sheep, and one of them has gone astray, does he not leave the ninety-nine on the hills and go in search of the one that went astray? [13]And if he finds it, truly, I say to you, he rejoices over it more than over the ninety-nine that never went astray.

[14]So it is not the will of my Father who is in heaven that one of these little ones should perish."

sheep, if he has lost one of them, does not leave the ninety-nine in the wilderness, and go after the one which is lost, until he finds it? [5]And when he has found it, he lays it on his shoulders, rejoicing. [6]And when he comes home, he calls together his friends and his neighbors, saying to them, 'Rejoice with me, for I have found my sheep which was lost.' [7]Just so, I tell you, there will be more joy in heaven over one sinner who repents than over ninety-nine righteous persons who need no repentance.

[8]Or what woman, having ten silver coins, if she loses one coin, does not light a lamp and sweep the house and seek diligently until she finds it? [9]And when she has found it, she calls together her friends and neighbors, saying 'Rejoice with me, for I have found the coin which I have lost.' [10]Just so, I tell you, there is joy before the angels of God over one sinner who repents."

In Luke's Gospel, these two similitudes present an interesting parallelism. The character in the Lost Sheep is a man, and in the Lost Coin a woman; the actions of both are worthy metaphors for God's saving activity. Both similitudes are introduced with a question beginning, "What man of you?" (v. 4), "Or what woman?" (v. 8); Jesus thus appeals to the hearers' own experience in order to win them over to a new view of the situation. Who among the hearers could deny that this is how they would act? The two similitudes have to do with the loss of a single sheep or coin, which the owner earnestly seeks, leaving for a while the safe ninety-nine or nine, until he or she finds the lost one and greatly rejoices.

Despite the fact that shepherds were regarded as dishonest, Jesus did not hesitate to use the figure of the shepherd in the first similitude to stand for God. A shepherd counts his flock every evening before putting them into the fold; this the shepherd has evidently just done. He seeks the one lost sheep not because it has great value, but simply because it has gone astray and cannot find its way back by itself. Since a lost sheep lies down, frightened and motionless, the shepherd must carry it back on his shoulders.

The emphasis is on the great joy of the shepherd on finding the lost sheep. He calls together his friends and neighbors to rejoice with him, probably at a feast. Just so will God rejoice over the sinner who repents.

In the second similitude it is a woman who stands for God. The coin was equivalent to a denarius; having only ten coins, the woman is poor. Here too the emphasis is on the joy at finding what was lost: the woman calls together her friends and neighbors to celebrate with her, most likely at a simple meal. Such will be God's joy over the repentant sinner.

Both similitudes end with a circumlocution for God, since emotion could not be ascribed to God; it is God who, at the last judgment (as indicated by the future tense) will rejoice over one sinner who returns. Jesus has illustrated the sinner's helplessness and God's concern. He thus hopes that his hearers have been led to adopt a fresh view of God's reign.

THE PRODIGAL SON

Lk 15:11–32

[11]And he said, "There was a man who had two sons;
[12]and the younger of them said to his father, 'Father, give
me the share of property that falls to me.' And he divided
his living between them. [13]Not many days later, the
younger son gathered all he had and took his journey into
a far country, and there he squandered his property in
loose living. [14]And when he had spent everything, a great
famine arose in that country, and he began to be in want.
[15]So he went and joined himself to one of the citizens of
that country, who sent him into his fields to feed swine.
[16]And he would gladly have fed on the pods that the swine
ate; and no one gave him anything. [17]But when he came to
himself he said, 'How many of my father's hired servants
have bread enough and to spare, but I perish here with
hunger! [18]I will arise and go to my father, and I will say to
him, 'Father, I have sinned against heaven and before
you; [19]I am no longer worthy to be called your son; treat
me as one of your hired servants.' [20]And he arose and
came to his father. But while he was yet at a distance, his
father saw him and had compassion, and ran and em-
braced him and kissed him. [21]And the son said to him,
'Father, I have sinned against heaven and before you; I
am no longer worthy to be called your son.' [22]But the
father said to his servants, 'Bring quickly the best robe,
and put it on him; and put a ring on his hand, and shoes on
his feet; [23]and bring the fatted calf and kill it, and let us eat
and make merry; [24]for this my son was dead, and is alive
again; he was lost, and is found.' And they began to make
merry.

[25]"Now his elder son was in the field; and as he came
and drew near to the house, he heard music and dancing.
[26]And he called one of the servants and asked what this
meant. [27]And he said to him, 'Your brother has come,

> and your father has killed the fatted calf, because he has received him safe and sound.' [28]But he was angry and refused to go in. His father came out and entreated him, [29]but he answered his father, 'Lo, these many years I have served you, and I never disobeyed your command; yet you never gave me a kid, that I might make merry with my friends. [30]But when this son of yours came, who has devoured your living with harlots, you killed for him the fatted calf!' [31]And he said to him, 'Son, you are always with me, and all that is mine is yours. [32]It was fitting to make merry and be glad, for this your brother was dead, and is alive; he was lost, and is found.'"

The parable of the Prodigal Son, certainly one of the most beautiful in the Gospels, has to do with God's concern for the sinner; the sinner's return; and the self-righteous person's resentment.

The parable is divided into two parts. The younger son is the protagonist in the first part; the elder son is the protagonist in the second part; the father is the protagonist throughout. Both parts end with the same exclamation, which expresses the point of the parable (as well as of the two preceeding similitudes).

The younger son, as was his legal right, asked for his share of the inheritance as a gift during his father's lifetime. He then left home and family. Like many Jews in that period, he sought his fortune in one of the countries of the Dispersion, that is, in the Greco-Roman world. His being lost and dead is related empathetically. Instead of finding his fortune, he wasted all his money, experienced a famine, and was forced to work with unclean animals (see Lev 11:7). Reduced to hunger, "he came to himself," that is, he repented. On his return, his father not only received him, but ran out to welcome him. The kiss was a sign of forgiveness (see 2 Sam 14:33). The father interrupted his son, and prevented him from asking to be treated as a servant (compare vv. 19 and 21); instead he gave orders for his full reinstatement as son. The fine robe (a mark of distinction), the ring (a signet ring, a sign of authority), and the shoes (worn only by free men), were tokens of the honor with which he was received (see Gen 41:42). The banquet was a sign of the son's return to the family table.

The elder son was resentful and resisted participating in the festivities. His situation, too, is described empathetically. His faithfulness is recognized by his father. The story ends with the father entreating him to join in rejoicing at his brother's homecoming. Whether or not he went in to the banquet is left an open question. He is not condemned.

This is a two-edged parable. The first part (like the preceding similitudes) justifies Jesus' mission to sinners. Not only is he who was lost now found (like the lost sheep and coin), but—what is far more wonderful—he who was dead is now alive (vv. 24 and 32). The second part of the parable is an invitation to those who have always been faithful. Their faithfulness is recognized by God, and his gifts are theirs, too. They are invited to cease murmuring at the way sinners are received and instead to rejoice in this good news. A repeated motif in this parable (as in the similitudes) is that of rejoicing (vv. 22–24, 25–27, 32). The banquet stands for both the joy at the end time and the Christian meal; both are celebrations of reconciliation and fellowship.

The parable as a whole is a splendid illustration of the way God acts. He is infinitely loving and boundlessly merciful. It is because God acts in this way that Jesus receives sinners.

E. The Great Feast; the Wedding Garment

THE GREAT FEAST AND THE WEDDING GARMENT

Mt 22:2–10; 11–14

[1]And again Jesus spoke to them in parables, saying, [2]"The kingdom of heaven

Lk 14:15–24

[16]But he said to him, "A man once gave a great banquet, and invited many;

may be compared to a king who gave a marriage feast for his son, [3]and sent his servants to call those who were invited to the marriage feast; but they would not come. [4]Again he sent other servants, saying, 'Tell those who are invited, Behold, I have made ready my dinner, my oxen and my fat calves are killed, and everything is ready; come to the marriage feast.' [5]But they made light of it and went off, one to his farm, another to his business, [6]while the rest seized his servants, treated them shamefully, and killed them. [7]The king was angry, and he sent his troops and destroyed those murderers and burned their city. [8]Then he said to his servants, 'The wedding is ready, but those invited were not worthy. [9]Go therefore to the thoroughfares, and invite to the marriage feast as many as you find.' [10]And those servants went out into the streets and gathered all whom they found, both bad and good; so the wedding hall was filled with guests.

[11]"But when the king came in to look at the guests, he saw there a man who had no wed-

[17] and at the time for the banquet he sent his servant to say to those who had been invited, 'Come; for all is now ready.' [18]But they all alike began to make excuses. The first said to him, 'I have bought a field, and I must go out and see it; I pray you, have me excused.' [19]And another said, 'I have bought five yoke of oxen, and I go to examine them; I pray you, have me excused.' [20]And another said, 'I have married a wife, and therefore I cannot come.' [21]So the servant came and reported this to his master. Then the householder in anger said to his servant, 'Go out quickly to the streets and lanes of the city, and bring in the poor and maimed and blind and lame.' [22]And the servant said, 'Sir, what you commanded has been done, and still there is room.' [23]And the master said to the servant, 'Go out to the highways and hedges, and compel people to come in, that my house may be filled. [24]For I tell you, none of those men who were invited shall taste my banquet.'"

ding garment; [12]and he said to him, 'Friend, how did you get in here without a wedding garment?' And he was speechless. [13]Then the king said to the attendants, 'Bind him hand and foot, and cast him into the outer darkness; there men will weep and gnash their teeth.' [14]For many are called, but few are chosen."

This parable is so different in its details in Matthew and Luke that it is not certain whether the evangelists received it from a common source, Q, or from two variant sources, M and L. (It is tentatively ascribed to the sayings-source Q in Appendix II of this book.) What is common to the Matthean and Lukan versions is the invited guests' refusal to attend the feast and their replacement by apparently less worthy types. Also, in both, the city stands for Israel and the feast for the messianic banquet or feast of salvation. Both interpret the parable as a missionary command. All of these common features are earlier than either Matthew or Luke.

In Luke's version, after the invited guests decline with various excuses, the servant is sent to convey the invitation to the uninvited twice (vv. 21 and 23; this occurs once in Matthew). The poor and the cripples brought in from "the streets and lanes of the city" no doubt stand for tax collectors and sinners in Israel. Those people brought in from "the highways and hedges" probably represent the Gentiles; Luke attached great importance to the Gentile mission. Luke's version is closer than Matthew's to the original.

Matthew has so edited this parable as to present it as a schematic outline of the history of salvation embracing the Israelite prophets, the Christian missionaries, the fall of Jerusalem, and the messianic banquet in the new age. The outline explains the shift of the mission from Israel, which rejected it, to the Gentiles. Whereas in Luke a "man" gives "a great banquet" (v. 16), in Matthew a "king" gives "a marriage feast for his son" (v. 2); the wedding feast was a traditional Jewish metaphor for the messianic banquet or feast of salvation. The single servant in Luke (vv. 17, 21–23) becomes two groups of servants in Matthew (vv. 3, 4); the first group is rejected (v. 3), the second is seized and killed (v. 6). The king, angered, sends his troops to destroy the murderers and burn their city (v. 7). He then sends his servants to "the thoroughfares" and "into the streets" (vv. 9–10a). Finally, the guests enter the wedding hall (v. 10b). Probably the first group of servants represents the prophets; the second group stands for the Christian apostles to Israel, or Jerusalem, some of whom were martyred; the expedition into the thoroughfares and streets stands for the Gentile mission; the destruction of the city and its inhabitants is an allusion to the fall of Jerusalem to the Romans in A.D. 70; and the entrance into the wedding hall represents baptism.

This parable is adressed to Jesus' critics and vindicates his mission to sinners against them. Since these opponents have rejected God's invitation, it has gone out to sinners and to Gentiles.

In Matthew, the conclusion (vv. 11–13) was probably originally a separate parable; it is often called the parable of the Wedding Garment. Matthew's purpose in conflating these two parables was to guard against the idea which might arise from the invitations to all without discrimination that one's conduct did not matter. Matthew wished to say that those admitted to baptism (v. 10b) were not excused from moral responsibility. Not all who are called will remain chosen.

8. THE CHALLENGE OF DISCIPLESHIP

JESUS' PREACHING is usually understood as having two major aspects: the eschatological and the ethical. Always the primary theme is the promise of salvation. In his eschatological message, Jesus proclaims the redemptive acts of God in history, what God does—the indicative. In his ethical teaching, Jesus sets down the principles of attitude and action which lead to eternal life, what persons must do—the imperative. He speaks of God's reign and God's will, the gift and the task. The two are interrelated: "You, therefore, must be perfect, as your heavenly Father is perfect" (Mt 5:48). In both, the immediacy of God's presence to us is revealed. God is our parent; we are to live as children of God. As one New Testament theologian has written, "God's goodness which encounters us is to be transposed into contemporary actualization" (Hans Conzelmann, *Jesus*).

The parables considered in this chapter belong to Jesus' ethical teaching. In them Jesus speaks of God's will, that is, of the requirements for discipleship.

A. The Treasure; the Pearl

In the parables of the Treasure and the Pearl, Jesus confronts his audience with the claims of God's reign. These parables are a challenge to decision. They pose the question whether the hearers are prepared to give all in order to gain the reign of God.

THE TREASURE AND THE PEARL

Mt 13:44, 45–46

> 44"The kingdom of heaven is like treasure hidden in a field, which a man found and covered up; then in his joy he goes and sells all that he has and buys that field.
>
> 45"Again, the kingdom of heaven is like a merchant in search of fine pearls, 46who, on finding one pearl of great value, went and sold all that he had and bought it.

These twin parables are preserved in Matthew's Gospel alone. They have the same introduction and are linked by the word "Again." In the second parable, the reign of God is compared, not to a merchant, but to a pearl. Both introductions could be translated: "It is the case with the reign of God as with. . . ."

In the first parable, the man simply stumbles upon the treasure; in the second, the merchant seeks before finding the pearl. Some interpreters think that Jesus had in mind the different ways by which persons come to the reign of God. Others see no significance in the different manner of discovery. The contrast may lie rather between the poor and the rich.

The first man is a poor farm worker. Hidden treasure is a frequent motif in the folk literature of the ancient Near East. In times of invasions and wars, the well-to-do often buried their valuables on their land; these sometimes remained in the earth until someone discovered them. This farm laborer, to his surprise and joy, comes upon such a cache (perhaps a jar containing money or jewelry). He buries the treasure again, in order both to leave it as a part of the field and to keep it safe. (According to rabbinic law, burying was considered the best security against theft.) A poor man, he must sell all that he has to buy the field; he knows that the treasure it holds is well worth the price.

The second man is a rich merchant. Pearls were very highly prized in antiquity. They were taken from the seas around the Near and Middle East and worn as adornment. The merchant has found an extraordinarily valuable pearl. He sells everything he has to buy the pearl; it is worth far more than all of his considerable holdings.

The emphasis in both parables is on the joy of discovering a thing of supreme value. These parables are not intended as a call to self-sacrifice; the stress is not on what must be given up in order to buy the valuable object. The point lies in the surpassing worth of the treasure compared to which all else seems worthless. The find is of such value that the discoverer, overjoyed, is glad to pay any price. This is how the true disciple responds to the discovery of the reign of God.

B. The Tower Builder; the Warring King

If the twin parables just discussed deal with the supreme value of the treasure of God's reign, the following twin similitudes speak of weighing the cost of making this treasure one's own.

THE TOWER BUILDER AND THE WARRING KING

Lk 14:28–30, 31–32

28 For which of you, desiring to build a tower, does not first sit down and count the cost, whether he has enough to complete it? 29 Otherwise, when he has laid a foundation, and is not able to finish, all who see it begin to mock him, 30 saying, 'This man began to build, and was not able to finish.'

> 31 Or what king, going to encounter another king in war, will not sit down first and take counsel whether he is able with ten thousand to meet him who comes against him with twenty thousand? 32 And if not, while the other is yet a great way off, he sends an embassy and asks terms of peace.

Many persons came to Jesus; he here warns them against undertaking discipleship lightly. To be a disciple of Jesus means to accept detachment and suffering. As the verse immediately preceding these similitudes reads: "Whoever does not bear his own cross and come after me, cannot be my disciple" (Lk 14:27). Yet to turn away from Jesus is to exclude oneself from the reign of God.

Jesus gives two illustrations of the need for careful assessment of the cost of discipleship: the farmer who, having failed to count the cost, is unable to finish the farm buildings and so becomes the object of ridicule, and the king who underestimates the enemy's strength and is consequently subject to the other's peace terms. Neither has taken the means to bring what he has started to completion. Jesus interprets the parables thus: "So therefore, whoever of you does not renounce all that he has cannot be my disciple" (v. 33).

C. The Unjust Steward; the Master and Servant

A characteristic required of the disciples of Jesus is prudence, wisdom, and decisive action in view of the coming of God's reign and the final judgment. Such a quality is portrayed in the following parable.

THE UNJUST STEWARD

Lk 16:1–8

> 1 He also said to the disciples, "There was a rich man who had a steward, and charges were brought to him that this man was wasting his goods. 2 And he called him and

said to him, 'What is this that I hear about you? Turn in the account of your stewardship, for you can no longer be steward.' [3]And the steward said to himself, 'What shall I do, since my master is taking the stewardship away from me? I am not strong enough to dig, and I am ashamed to beg. [4]I have decided what to do, so that people may receive me into their houses when I am put out of the stewardship. [5]So, summoning his master's debtors one by one, he said to the first, 'How much do you owe my master?' [6]He said, 'A hundred measures of oil.' And he said to him, 'Take your bill, and sit down quickly and write fifty.' [7]Then he said to another, 'And how much do you owe?' He said, 'A hundred measures of wheat.' He said to him, 'Take your bill, and write eighty.' [8]The master commended the dishonest steward for his prudence; for the sons of this world are wiser in their own generation than the sons of light.

This parable was probably originally addressed to a general audience, and not to the disciples, as its Lukan context says (v. 1); its theme, namely, foresight and decisive action in view of the impending crisis of the final judgment, seems intended for hearers who are not heeding Jesus' announcement of the coming of God's reign.

The steward, or manager, of an estate is accused of wasting his master's goods; he has betrayed the commission entrusted to him. He is therefore dismissed from his position. The steward meets this crisis by calling in his master's debtors and having them rewrite their promissory notes for lesser amounts. He hopes that the debtors will in turn care for him; he thus takes steps to secure his future. The master commends the steward for his prudent and resolute action in the face of this crisis. The parable's lesson is that the hearers ought to imitate his worldly wisdom with an other-worldy wisdom. They, too, may have betrayed the commission entrusted to them; they must now take prudent and resolute action in view of the coming crisis of the final judgment.

The exegesis of this parable is fraught with difficulties. A much disputed question is whether the "master" in v. 8a, who commends the steward, is the rich man in the parable or Jesus. That is, does v. 8a belong to the parable itself or to the commentary appended to it? Linked to this question is the interpretation of the entire parable.

Interpreters have long thought that the master in v. 8a was Jesus; the parable would thus end with v. 7. In the parable itself the steward is apparently dishonest, or unjust, on two counts: for having wasted his master's goods, as related in v. 1; and for having falsified his accounts, as narrated in vv. 5–7. It is for the latter that the master commends the steward in v. 8a. The owner of the estate could not possibly praise his steward for falsifying the accounts; the master in v. 8a must therefore be Jesus. That the steward was acting wrongfully in vv. 5–7 is of no consequence for the parable's meaning; it is only his resourcefulness which Jesus holds up as a model for his audience.

Another interpretation has recently found wide acceptance among exegetes. It is noted that if the master in v. 8a is Jesus, and this verse belongs to the commentary, then the parable itself has no real conclusion. It is more likely that the master is the owner of the estate and the parable ends with v. 8a. The parable comprises vv. 1–8a, the commentary vv. 8b–13.

On this interpretation, the steward, in vv. 5–7, is acting in accordance with the law; indeed nothing in these verses indicates that the steward is committing any wrongdoing. This interpretation is based on laws of agency and usury in the rabbinic literature. The steward, as his master's agent, was legally authorized to act in his master's name; the steward's accounts were not subject to audit, until he left his position. He had the legal power to carry out all the actions assumed in the parable. The steward had acted dishonestly *before* the story: on each debtor's bill he had recorded the principal owed to the master *plus* an interest to be paid to himself—despite the fact that usury was forbidden by Jewish law. (He had employed a common way of evading the law. By writing the bills in terms of oil and wheat rather than money, such businessmen observed the letter but not the spirit of the law prohibiting usury.) The steward thus realized an illegal gain. Now, faced with the loss of his position, he must act to extricate himself from his predicament; he has the debtors reduce the amounts owed, not by reducing the principal, but simply by cancelling the interest they would have paid to him. Thus, it is precisely in vv. 5–7 that the steward is observing the law: the unlawful usury and graft committed earlier is now undone. The master is cast in a good light, as a man who upholds the law against usury; he ratifies the steward's transactions and praises him for his prudence.

The point of the parable: if the steward, who is wise in the ways of the world, has the resourcefulness to undo his illegal actions and remain in the good graces of his neighbors, how much more should the hearers, who ought to be wise in an other-worldly sense, have the prudence to amend their lives and remain in the good graces of God.

In the Gospel, a series of four separate applications, all secondary, is appended to the parable on the basis of catchwords (vv. 8b, 9, 10–12, 13). We have here an interesting example of modifications made in the interpretation of a parable during the course of transmission. These are discussed above, in Chapter 5, Section B.

The most basic characteristic required of the followers of Jesus is the willingness to serve God selflessly. This requirement is the subject of the following little similitude.

THE MASTER AND SERVANT

Lk 17:7–10

7 "Will any one of you, who has a servant plowing or keeping sheep, say to him when he has come in from the field, 'Come at once and sit down at table'? 8 Will he not rather say to him, 'Prepare supper for me, and gird yourself and serve me, till I eat and drink; and afterward

> you shall eat and drink'? [9]Does he thank the servant because he did what was commanded? [10]So you also, when you have done all that is commanded you, say, 'We are unworthy servants: we have only done what was our duty.'"

This similitude, preserved by Luke alone, begins, "Will any of you?"; it derives its persuasiveness from the appeal to the hearers' experience. It is not possible to determine whether it was originally addressed to the disciples, as Luke has it, or to a general audience.

A servant's work belongs to his master, and a day's work is no more than a servant's duty. The servant who does his daily work has no claim on his master's special gratitude. So it is with the servants of God; they are called to obedience to God's will. The servants of God who perform their duty, fulfilling God's will, should not think that they have done more, and expect a special recompense. God will reward precisely the one who serves without thought of reward.

The similitude may originally have been a criticism of the legalistic mentality preoccupied with the idea of merit.

D. The Friend at Midnight; the Persistent Widow

The following similitude and parable have to do with prayer. In them Jesus exhorts his hearers to have faith and hope that God will answer their prayers.

THE FRIEND AT MIDNIGHT

Lk 11:5–8

> [5]And he said to them, "Which of you who has a friend will go to him at midnight and say to him, 'Friend, lend me three loaves; [6]for a friend of mine has arrived on a journey, and I have nothing to set before him'; [7]and he

> will answer from within, 'Do not bother me; the door is now shut, and my children are with me in bed; I cannot get up and give you anything'? [8]I tell you, though he will not get up and give him anything because he is his friend, yet because of his importunity he will rise and give him whatever he needs.

This similitude, which Luke has preserved, begins, "Which of you?" It thus appeals to the hearers' own experience. No one would deny that this is how they would act in a similar situation.

The similitude accurately reflects life in an ancient village of Palestine. The homemaker bakes the family's daily bread before dawn. Entertainment of a guest is an important obligation. The main character has nothing to offer his guest, who has arrived unexpectedly; he wants to borrow from his friend three loaves (the portion for one person) which he will immediately replace. But it is midnight; the friend and his family are asleep. Perhaps we are to think of a one-room house in which parents and children all sleep together on a mat in one part of the room. The door has been bolted with a large bar placed through slots; its removal would inconvenience the owner and probably awaken everyone. The friend, hardly anxious to disturb himself and his family, at first resists the request; but he eventually accedes, if only because of his friend's importunity, and gives him what he needs.

The similitude occurs in the context of a Lukan section on prayer (11:1–13). It is bracketed by the Lord's Prayer (11:2–4) and this saying: "And I tell you, Ask, and it will be given you; seek, and you will find; knock, and it will be opened to you. For every one who asks receives, and he who seeks finds, and to him who knocks it will be opened" (11:9–10). The motif of bread, a metaphor for all our needs, links this similitude to the Lord's Prayer, which precedes it; the motif of knocking on the door, a metaphor for prayer, links the similitude to the saying which follows it.

The similitude employs the argument from the lesser to the greater: if this man who has good reason to reject his friend's request is nevertheless moved to do what his friend asks, how much more will God give to you all that you need. The lesson is that God will respond without fail to those who pray with perseverance. The emphasis is less on the need for persistence in prayer than on the certainty that God will answer. God is one who hears our requests and gives us even more than we need. The similitude exhorts the hearers to faith and hope.

THE PERSISTENT WIDOW

Lk 18:1–8

> [1]And he told them a parable, to the effect that they ought always to pray and not lose heart. [2]He said, "In a certain city there was a judge who neither feared God nor regarded man; [3]and there was a widow in that city who kept coming to him and saying, 'Vindicate me against my adversary.' [4]For a while he refused; but afterward he said to himself, 'Though I neither fear God nor regard man, [5]yet because this widow bothers me, I will vindicate her, or she will wear me out by her continual coming.'" [6]And the Lord said, "Hear what the unrighteous judge says. [7]And will not God vindicate his elect, who cry to him day and night? Will he delay long over them? [8]I tell you, he will vindicate them speedily. Nevertheless, when the Son of man comes, will he find faith on earth?"

This parable is closely parallel to the similitude of the Friend at Midnight. It immediately precedes the exemplary story of the Pharisee and the Tax Collector (18:9–14); together these two stories illustrate the right attitude in prayer: the widow exemplifies perseverance, the tax collector humility.

On the literal level of the story, this woman, a widow, belongs to one of the marginalized and oppressed groups. These are the ones whom the Bible calls "the poor"—the economically poor, women, orphans, prisoners, the sick, and the like. They stand powerless before the legal, social, and religious structures. As Psalm 146 says, the poor are the special objects of God's concern; he "executes justice for the oppressed" (Ps 146:7). The widow's adversary is probably a powerful and wealthy man. The only course of action open to her is persistence. At first the judge rejects her demand for vindication; but finally her perseverance prevails.

The widow stands for all those who "hunger and thirst for righteousness" (Mt 5:6); the judge stands for God. This parable, like its parallel, the Friend at Midnight, employs the argument from the lesser to the greater: if this judge, to whom justice means little, finally vindicates the widow, how much more will God vindicate those who seek justice. As in the Friend at Midnight, the emphasis is on the certainty that God answers those who persist in prayer.

The story of this woman is an encouragement to those who suffer injustice in society and the Church; provided they do not lose heart, God will certainly "execute justice" on their behalf.

The parable is reminiscent of a passage in Sirach:

> for the Lord is the judge, and with him is no partiality.
> 13 He will not show partiality in the case of a poor man; and he will listen to the prayer of one who is wronged.
> 14 He will not ignore the supplication of the fatherless, nor the widow when she pours out her story,
> 15 Do not the tears of the widow run down her cheek as she cries out against him who has caused them to fall?
> 16 He whose service is pleasing to the Lord will be accepted, and his prayer will reach to the clouds.
>
> (Sir 35:12b–16)

E. *The Unmerciful Servant; the Good Samaritan*

Central to the Gospel is the assurance of the divine forgiveness; Jesus himself mediated God's forgiveness to all those who came to him. But this incredible gift is one we must share. A characteristic required of those who would be Jesus' disciples is a forgiving spirit: "Be merciful, even as your Father is merciful" (Lk 6:36). This is the lesson of the remarkable story of the Unmerciful Servant.

THE UNMERCIFUL SERVANT

Mt 18:23–35

> [23]"Therefore the kingdom of heaven may be compared to a king who wished to settle accounts with his servants. [24]When he began the reckoning, one was brought to him who owed him ten thousand talents; [25]and as he could not pay, his lord ordered him to be sold, with his wife and children and all that he had, and payment to be made. [26]So the servant fell on his knees, imploring him, 'Lord, have patience with me, and I will pay you everything.' [27]And out of pity for him the lord of that servant released him and forgave him the debt. [28]But that same servant, as he went out, came upon one of his fellow servants who owed him a hundred denarii; and seizing him by the throat he said, 'Pay what you owe.' [29]So his fellow servant fell down and besought him, 'Have patience with me, and I will pay you.' [30]He refused and went and put him in prison till he should pay the debt. [31]When his fellow servants saw what had taken place, they were greatly distressed, and they went and reported to their lord all that had taken place. [32]Then his lord summoned him and said to him, 'You wicked servant! I forgave you all that debt because you besought me; [33]and should not you have had mercy on your fellow servant, as I had mercy on you?' [34]And in anger his lord delivered him to the jailers, till he should pay all his debt. [35]So also my heavenly Father will do to every one of you, if you do not forgive your brother from your heart.

Though the parable begins, "the kingdom of heaven may be compared to a king," the coming of God's reign is compared rather to a reckoning (as in the Laborers in the Vineyard). The preceding question of Peter, "Lord, how often shall my brother sin against me, and I forgive him?" and Jesus' answer, "seventy times seven" (Mt 18:21–22), is probably a secondary setting for the parable. The parable does not illustrate forgiveness an unlimited number of times; it portrays, not repeated, but boundless forgiveness.

The "king" is a standard Jewish metaphor for God. The "king's servants," in the Bible and in the ancient Near East, are his high officials; they here stand for the hearers of the parable. The magnitude of the amount which the official owed the king suggests that he was a satrap responsible for the revenue from his province. The amount owed, ten thousand talents, is fantastic; the figure is meant to be beyond grasp (in the biblical world, ten thousand is the highest number used in reckoning, and the talent is the largest denomination). It is in sharp contrast to the small amount of one hundred denarii (a denarius was the usual wage for a day's labor). The sum owed is so great that it could not possibly be either repaid or restored by the sale of the servant, his family, and his property; the sale is meant rather as a punishment and a warning to others. The king and his officials are probably Gentiles: Jewish law prohibited the sale of an Israelite man except in case of a theft when what was stolen could not be restored, and it prohibited the sale of a wife in any case. The situation of the official and his family is desperate. His prostration is an expression of his desperation, as is his plea for mercy; his promise to pay the debt is meaningless. The king hears the official's plea; since payment is out of the question, the king simply cancels the entire debt. His mercy far transcends the official's plea.

The official, going out, then encounters a fellow official who owes him the trivial amount of one hundred denarii. The prostration and plea for mercy of the second official are identical to that of the first—except that this time the promise of repayment could be kept. But the first official, unlike the king, does not hear, having failed to learn the lesson of mercy. The second official is not sold, since that was done only when the debt was greater than the amount to be realized from the sale of the debtor. Instead the debtor is imprisoned, until he or his family find a means of paying the debt.

Other officials, shocked at what has taken place, report it to the king. The king denounces the official: "should not you have had mercy on your fellow servant, as I had mercy on you?" (v. 33). The question is addressed to all who hear the parable. The official is imprisoned just as he had imprisoned his fellow official; but in his case, since the debt can never be paid, the punishment is eternal.

We are given an explicit interpretation of the parable: "So also my heavenly Father will do to every one of you, if you do not forgive your brother from your heart" (v. 35). Forgiveness from the heart is in contrast to forgiveness with the lips only; forgiveness must be sincere. Having freely received forgiveness for our offenses against the infinite God, we have an obligation freely to extend forgiveness for the trivial offenses of our fellow human beings against us. Unless we grant forgiveness to others, God will on the last day revoke the forgiveness he has granted to us. The parable thus conveys, not only an exhortation, but a warning concerning the last judgment.

Forgiveness and love are interrelated. For Jesus, the double commandment of love of God and neighbor supersedes and includes all other commandments (Mk 12:28–34; Mt 2:34–40; Lk 10:25–28). Love is therefore the most important quality required of the disciples of Jesus. This quality is portrayed in the exemplary story of the Good Samaritan.

THE GOOD SAMARITAN

Lk 10:29–37

> 29 But he, desiring to justify himself, said to Jesus, "And who is my neighbor?" 30 Jesus replied, "A man was

> going down from Jerusalem to Jericho, and he fell among
> robbers, who stripped him and beat him, and departed,
> leaving him half dead. 31 Now by chance a priest was going
> down that road; and when he saw him he passed by on the
> other side. 32 So likewise a Levite, when he came to the
> place and saw him, passed by on the other side. 33 But a
> Samaritan, as he journeyed, came to where he was; and
> when he saw him, he had compassion, 34 and went to him
> and bound up his wounds, pouring on oil and wine; then
> he set him on his own beast and brought him to an inn,
> and took care of him. 35 And the next day he took out two
> denarii and gave them to the innkeeper, saying, 'Take
> care of him; and whatever more you spend, I will repay
> you when I come back.' 36 Which of these three, do you
> think, proved neighbor to the man who fell among the
> robbers?" 37 He said, "The one who showed mercy on
> him." And Jesus said to him, "Go and do likewise."

Surely the exemplary story of the Good Samaritan ranks as one of the most beautiful and compelling of all the Synoptic parables. It illustrates the teaching of Jesus on love of God and neighbor; there is nothing more central in Jesus' preaching. Indeed, love is all that is necessary for eternal life (Lk 10:28).

A word is in order concerning the passage introducing this parable in Luke's Gospel (Lk 10:25–28; Mk 12:28–34 and Mt 22:34–40 may be parallels to this passage, although the differences make this uncertain). A lawyer—that is, a scribe, one learned in the Scriptures and the Law—asks Jesus, a layman, "Teacher, what shall I do to inherit eternal life?" (Lk 10:25). Jesus invites the lawyer himself to cite the law, namely, the double commandment to love God and neighbor (Dt 6:5; Lev 19:18). Perhaps the lawyer knew that Jesus preached the primacy of love repeatedly. Jesus affirms the lawyer's response. "Do this," Jesus says, "and you will live" (v. 28); the scribe's theological knowledge will gain him nothing unless he puts the double commandment into practice. But the lawyer now poses a casuistic question. He wishes to "justify" himself, that is, perhaps, to show that he has observed this law within its recognized limits. "And who is my neighbor?" (v. 29), he asks. This was a disputed question: all agreed that the term "neighbor" included compatriots; but the term was thought also to exclude certain groups, such as non-Pharisees (by the Pharisees), the "sons of darkness" (by the Essenes), heretics, and the like (see Mt 5:43–48). The scribe asks Jesus to define the limits of his responsibility. Jesus' answer is the story of the Good Samaritan; in it he shows that one who loves seeks not limits but opportunity.

A knowledge of who the characters are enriches our understanding of the exemplary story. The priests were the officials of the Temple (which was located in Jerusalem); they were the highest religious leaders in Israel. The Levites were the associates of the priests in the Temple. The Samaritans were a people who were mixed both ethnically and religiously. These people, who lived in the central part of Palestine, were the descendants of marriages between Israelites and foreign colonists brought into the region after the Assyrian conquest of Israel in 722 B.C. The Samaritans' religion, similar to the Jews', nevertheless differed from it in several significant respects (see John 4). The Samaritans were, strictly speaking, neither Jews nor Gentiles. They were regarded by the Jews as a half-breed and religiously impure people. The Jews did not speak to the Samaritans; certainly a Samaritan would not be expected to show compassion to a Jew.

Even today the traveler on the road from Jerusalem to Jericho, seventeen miles northeast, is in danger of being robbed. It is not made clear whether the priest and Levite were simply callous or whether, thinking that the unconscious man was dead, they observed the prescription forbidding a priest to defile himself by touching a dead body (except that of a near kin; Lev 21:1–3). Oil and wine were used medicinally: oil to mollify (Isa. 1:6) and wine to disinfect. The Samaritan was perhaps a merchant who often traveled the road, since he seems to be acquainted with the innkeeper. Following the first two passers-by, a Jewish priest and Levite, the hearers may have expected as the third passer-by a Jewish layman. To hear that the one who fulfilled the commandment of love was a Samaritan would have shocked the audience. Jesus deliberately depicts the two extremes: the Jewish servants of God and the heretical Samaritan layman. Thus does Jesus stunningly convey the absolute and boundless requirement to love the neighbor.

Much exegetical discussion revolves around Jesus' concluding question: "Which of these three, do you think, proved neighbor to the man who fell among the robbers?" (v. 36). It is sometimes objected that Jesus has failed to answer the lawyer's question. The lawyer asked (v. 29) about the object of love (Whom must I treat as a neighbor?); Jesus asks (v. 36) about the subject of love (Who has acted as a neighbor?). Yet Jesus has in fact directly addressed the question: the lawyer asked Jesus to define the limits of his responsibility in observing the law; Jesus replies that the duty to love is without limits. The term "neighbor" includes one's compatriots but, as the example of the Samaritan shows, it can never be limited to that. There is no case in which the law of love is not to be observed. The double commandment of love was not new with Jesus; he derived it from the Old Testament (Dt 6:5; Lev 19:18). But Jesus preached its absoluteness. Jesus' final saying, "God and do likewise" (v. 37) repeats emphatically his saying preceding the parable, "do this, and you will live" (v. 28). As has been observed in Chapter 7, Jesus himself enacted what he here preached by associating with those marginalized by society and religion.

In the exemplary story, the priest and Levite represent those who are officially religious but who fail to observe the commandment to love one's neighbor; the Samaritan stands for those who are outside the official circle of God's people but who nevertheless truly do God's will; and the wounded man represents anyone in need. The meaning of the exemplary story is that official membership and even high position in the established religion can be no substitute for the concrete deed of love for someone in need. This is a hard lesson for some to hear, but one of supreme importance.

Throughout the Gospels we see contrasted two ways of being religious: on the one hand, the hollow conformity to traditions and laws, largely man-made, which Jesus criticized (see, for example, Mark 7), and on the other hand, the radical understanding of God's will which Jesus preached. This exemplary story depicts brilliantly the contrast between the two.

F. The Two Builders

THE TWO BUILDERS

Mt 7:24–27; Lk 6:47–49

24 "Every one then who
hears these words of mine and
does them will be like a wise
man who built
his house
upon the
rock; 25 and the
rain fell, and the floods came,
and the winds blew and beat
upon that house, but it did not
fall, because it had been
founded on the rock. 26 And
everyone who hears these words
of mine and does not do them
will be like a foolish man who
built his house upon the sand;
27 and the rain fell, and the
floods came, and the winds blew
and beat against that house, and

47 "Every one who comes to
me and hears my words and
does them, I will show you what
he is like: 48 he is like a man
building a house, who dug deep,
and laid the foundation upon
rock; and when a
flood arose, the stream broke
against that house, and could
not shake it, because it had been
well built.

49 But he who hears
and does not do them
is like a man who
built a house on the ground
without a foundation; against
which the stream broke, and
immediately

it fell; and great was the fall of it."	it fell, and the ruin of that house was great."

The great sermon of Jesus, in both Matthew's and Luke's Gospels (the Sermon on the Mount in Matthew 5–7; the Sermon on the Plain in Lk 6:17–49), concludes with the similitude of the Two Builders. The sermon, including this ending, was preserved in Q. Matthew's version of the similitude, it will be noted, is the more vividly told.

The reader may be interested in comparing this Synoptic similitude with the rabbinic parallel which is quoted in Chapter 1 of this book. The image in the rabbinic story is a tree and its roots, and in the Synoptic story a house and its foundation; but the point of the two stories is much the same.

Jesus has laid down, in his sermon, the ethical principles of life under God's reign. He has outlined the attitudes and actions demanded of his followers. He brings the sermon to a close with this similitude, which emphasizes the point that we must not only hear but also do these words; we are to live them.

This similitude is one of the easiest of the Synoptic parables to interpret. Building a house on rock stands for both hearing and doing the words of Jesus; building a house on sand stands for hearing them only. The storm probably represents the severe trials in the life of a disciple. We must not only listen to but also put into practice what Jesus says. In times of testing, only the solid foundation of obedience to Jesus' words will provide the security that will enable us to weather the crisis. A life of merely superficial assent to Jesus' words will end in tragedy.

The similitude of the Two Builders has much the same lesson as the parable of the Sower: it is not enough merely to receive the word; it must be kept and nurtured through trials and tribulations of all kinds (Mk 4:14–19). As noted above, at the end of Chapter 4, truly to understand the parables and the other words of Jesus is to obey them; hearing *is* doing.

This similitude is one of those important for its indirect christology. We have here an extraordinary claim: it is Jesus who lays down the ethical principles which are the conditions for life under the reign of God. Our eternal life depends on hearing and doing *Jesus'* words: "these words of *mine*." As Matthew says in conclusion, the crowds were astonished at Jesus' sermon, "for he taught them as one who had authority, and not as their scribes" (Mt 7:28–29). Jesus' authority rests not only on an appeal to the Scriptures, as did that of the scribes; his authority derives from his own radical understanding of God's will. Jesus claims an authority greater even than that of any prophet. And this design for life which Jesus gives is the only one that will last.

9. THE CALL TO REPENTANCE

THE LAST GROUP of parables has to do with the eschatological crisis. Jesus proclaimed the coming of God's reign: his message was an announcement not only of salvation but also of judgment. The final judgment would take place with the establishment of God's reign in power and glory. Repeatedly Jesus warned of the approaching crisis and called both the religious leaders and the people to repentance. In a number of parables, he tried to awaken his audience to the seriousness of the moment. He attempted to warn those who were spiritually blind, deaf, and hard of heart, who refused to allow the eschatological crisis in the future to impinge upon their existence in the present. The parables considered in this chapter are a cry of warning and a call to repentance in view of the final judgment.

The early Church handed on these parables and incorporated them into the Gospels in the time between the first and second advents of Jesus Christ, between his death and resurrection and his expected return on the clouds as Son of Man and judge (see Mk 14:62; 8:38–9:1). The term for the second coming of Jesus Christ at the end of history is the Greek word parousia, which means "presence." The early Church adapted a few of these parables to its own situation, interpreting them as parables about the parousia; these are the Ten Maidens, the Talents or Pounds, and the

Faithful or Unfaithful Servant. They provide an interesting example of modifications in the parables made by the early Church.

A. The Rich Fool; the Ten Maidens

In the parables of the Rich Fool and the Ten Maidens, Jesus' aim is to awaken people to the approaching crisis. In the former, he tries to overcome his hearers' obduracy, warning them of possible impending catastrophe; in the latter, he admonishes them to be prepared.

THE RICH FOOL

Lk 12:16–21

> 16 And he told them a parable, saying, "The land of a rich man brought forth plentifully; 17 and he thought to himself, 'What shall I do, for I have nowhere to store my crops?' 18 And he said, 'I will do this: I will pull down my barns, and build larger ones; and there I will store all my grain and my goods. 19 And I will say to my soul, Soul, you have ample goods laid up for many years; take your ease, eat, drink, be merry.' 20 But God said to him, 'Fool! This night your soul is required of you; and the things you have prepared, whose will they be?' 21 So is he who lays up treasure for himself, and is not rich toward God."

It is not at all certain that the introductory incident in Luke's Gospel (12:13–15) preserves the original occasion of this exemplary story. Some such occurrence, however, must be assumed as the setting of the parable. A man asks Jesus to settle his dispute with his brother concerning their inheritance. That the man appeals to Jesus, a layman, shows the high regard in which Jesus was held. Jesus refuses to act as arbiter, not because he lacks the authority, but because the possession of property has nothing to do with the reign of

God. Instead he responds that life does not consist in the abundance of possessions (v. 15). Jesus thus changes the subject from possessions to one's attitude toward them. He tells the story of the rich fool to illustrate his point that possessions are not to be confounded with life.

The most striking feature of this exemplary story is its sudden climax. We are shown a picture of a life of prosperity and pleasure. A wealthy landowner is absorbed in earning money and making plans for the future. He has received abundant harvests and need not fear the failure of crops for many years. He devotes himself to providing for a future of ease and enjoyment. Then death strikes with appalling swiftness; there is no future. God takes this man by surprise, ending all in one night.

The exemplary story is not, as we might think, a lesson against greed. Neither is it teaching about the suddenness of death. Jesus here points to the last judgment. The exemplary story is best understood as a warning to the hearers to open their eyes to the approaching crisis. The rich farmer is called a "fool" in the biblical sense, as a person who says in his or her heart, "There is no God" (Ps 14:1; see also Ps 10:4, 11; 94:7). Such persons deny for all practical purposes the existence of God.

V. 21 is a generalizing conclusion added secondarily. It changes the thrust of the exemplary story from an eschatological warning to a moral teaching on the wrong use of possessions.

THE TEN MAIDENS

Mt 25:1–13

1"Then the kingdom of heaven shall be compared to
ten maidens who took their lamps and went to meet the
bridegroom. 2Five of them were foolish, and five were
wise. 3For when the foolish took their lamps, they took
no oil with them; 4but the wise took flasks of oil with

their lamps. [5]As the bridegroom was delayed, they all slumbered and slept. [6]But at midnight there was a cry, 'Behold, the bridegroom! Come out to meet him.' [7]Then all those maidens rose and trimmed their lamps. [8]And the foolish said to the wise, 'Give us some of your oil, for our lamps are going out.' [9]But the wise replied, 'Perhaps there will not be enough for us and for you; go rather to the dealers and buy for yourselves.' [10]And while they went to buy, the bridegroom came, and those who were ready went in with him to the marriage feast; and the door was shut. [11]Afterward the other maidens came also, saying, 'Lord, lord, open to us.' [12]But he replied, 'Truly, I say to you, I do not know you.' [13]Watch therefore, for you know neither the day nor the hour."

The parable of the Ten Maidens appears in Matthew's Gospel alone. It may have been addressed by Jesus to a general audience. The "kingdom of heaven" is compared, not to ten maidens (v. 1), but to all that is narrated about the wedding festivities.

Certain features of this narrative of a wedding strike us as odd; some interpreters have argued against the authenticity of the parable on the grounds that the events depicted here do not belong to an ordinary wedding. Other commentators, however, argue that the story accurately depicts a wedding in ancient Palestine. They maintain that the marriage feast at night, the meeting of the bridegroom with lamps, and the bridegroom's delay are all authentic features.

Little is known about first-century Palestinian wedding customs. Jeremias gives two examples of modern weddings in Israel which shed some light on this parable. In the villages, after a day of celebration, the marriage feast takes place in the evening. Then the bride is escorted by torchlight to the bridegroom's house. Later the bridegroom's arrival is announced; the women leave the bride and go out with torches to greet and escort the bridegroom. In a Jerusalem wedding, the festivities take place during the evening in the bride's house. Then, late at night and after repeated announcements, the bridegroom comes for her; he is accompanied by his friends with lamps, and is greeted by the bride's guests. All then proceed, again with lamps, to the house of the bridegroom's parents where the marriage ceremony takes place. It is customary for the bridegroom to negotiate with the bride's relatives over the gifts he gives them. The bargaining shows that the relatives do not easily part with the bride. It is the length of this transaction that occasionally causes the delay of the bridegroom.

The parable, then, is realistic. The wedding festivities, and especially the procession by torchlight, are joyous events. The ten maidens are the attendants who greet and accompany the bridegroom. In a device characteristic of the parables, the maidens are divided into two groups, five "wise" and five "foolish." The foolish maidens neglect to take extra oil for their lamps; they are too shortsighted to anticipate the possibility of the bridegroom's delay. The wise ones have foresight and prepare for the possibility by bringing extra oil. It is late, and when the bridegroom is indeed delayed, all the maidens doze off. They are awakened at midnight by the announcement of the bridegroom's arrival. They hasten to prepare their lamps, trimming the burnt wicks and filling them with oil so that they can burn brightly. The foolish ask to borrow oil from the wise, but the wise refuse. If the limited supply of oil is shared, all of them may run out, and there will be no torchlight at all for the procession. The foolish attendants are guilty, not of falling asleep, for the wise ones have also slept, but of failing to provide oil for their lamps. While the foolish ones go off to buy oil, the bridegroom arrives, and the wise ones accompany him into the wedding feast. The foolish maidens return only to find the door shut and bolted; they plead for admission to the feast, but the bridegroom responds that he will have nothing to do with them (v. 12). (Possibly the maidens are servants belonging to the household of the bride's parents.) For the foolish, a joyous event ends in disaster.

On the lips of Jesus, the parable exhorts the hearers to be prepared for the eschatological hour. The parable begins on a joyous note (v. 1). The maidens represent the hearers of the parable. The sudden arrival of the bridegroom (v. 6) stands for the unexpected eschatological crisis. The wedding feast stands for the feast of salvation or the messianic banquet, the consummation of God's reign. The parable of the Ten Maidens warns the hearers not to be, as were the foolish maidens, imprudent and unprepared; they will find themselves excluded from the reign of God. It is at the door that the judgment takes place. The parable ends on a tragic note. The door is closed; those who are unprepared are shut out; it is too late—the judgment against them is irrevocable (vv. 10–12). The parable, then, speaks of those who are prepared and those who are unprepared, and of their separation at the final judgment. Being prudent and prepared means living a life of faith and good works in the present, in view of final judgment in the future—which comes no one knows when.

In the early Church and in the Gospel of Matthew, the parable is understood as having to do with the delay of the parousia, or second coming of Jesus Christ. The "then" in v. 1 refers to the parousia, as does the command in v. 13. The bridegroom, called "Lord" in v. 11, stands for the Messiah. The meaning is essentially unchanged, however, since the parousia is one aspect of the eschatological event. The ten maidens now represent the Christian community. The emphasis is placed on the delay of the parousia; the tarrying of the bridegroom in v. 5 receives special stress. The parable is made to address what was perhaps a problem in Matthew's community or in the early Church: foolish unconcern about the interval of time before the parousia. The main point of the parable is still the inexorable separation of the wise and the foolish, the prepared and the unprepared, at the judgment.

Whether v. 13 is an original part of the parable is a question. All ten maidens, wise and foolish, fall asleep; then, if the command to "watch" is a warning to remain awake or alert in view of the unknown hour of the eschatological crisis, the verse does not fit the parable. It could belong to the original parable only if "watch" means "be prudent, be ready, be prepared."

B. The Barren Fig Tree; the Rich Man and Lazarus

The parables of the Barren Fig Tree and the Rich Man and Lazarus are a warning about the judgment. In them, Jesus tells his hearers that unless they repent God's judgment will surely fall.

THE BARREN FIG TREE

Lk 13:6–9

> [6]And he told this parable: "A man had a fig tree planted in his vineyard; and he came seeking fruit on it and found none. [7]And he said to the vinedresser, 'Lo, these three years I have come seeking fruit on this fig tree, and I find none. Cut it down; why should it use up the ground?' [8]And he answered him, 'Let it alone, sir, this year also, till I dig about it and put on manure. [9]And if it bears fruit next year, well and good; but if not, you can cut it down.'"

The parable of the Barren Fig Tree is preserved in Luke alone. It is possible, though not certain, that the story of Jesus' cursing of the fig tree found in Mark and Matthew (Mk 11:12–14; Mt 21:18–22) is a creation based on this parable.

When a new fig tree was planted, it was allowed to grow for three years before its fruit was plucked (Lev 19:23); in this story, yet another three years have elapsed. In the owner's judgment, the tree is hopelessly barren. A fig tree draws much nourishment from the earth which would otherwise go to the sustenance of the surrounding vines; therefore an unfruitful fig tree cannot simply be permitted to stand. The owner pronounces the sentence: the tree is to be cut down. The vinedresser makes an appeal: he pleads for a reprieve of one year—the absolute limit—during which he will make every effort to save the tree. The Old Testament nowhere mentions the fertilizing of a vineyard with manure; neither does a fig tree require this. The vinedresser is here offering to give the tree extraordinary care. It is understood that the owner grants the vinedresser's request. The sentence already pronounced is now suspended. Justice is tempered with mercy.

In this story the owner stands for God and the fig tree for the people; also, according to many (though not all) exegetes, the vinedresser stands for Jesus. The people have no cause to be complacent. In God's eyes, they are morally sterile. God requires of persons that they "bear fruit"; the fruits stand for justice and righteousness. This is a metaphor with a long tradition in the Old Testament and Jewish literature (see Is 5:7; Jer 2:21; Hos 10:1); it is taken over in the New Testament (see Mt 3:8–10; 7:16–20; 12:33; Lk 6:43–45). Elsewhere in Luke's Gospel we read this utterance of John the Baptist, which resembles the parable:

> 8Bear fruits that befit repentance, and do not begin to say to yourselves, 'We have Abraham as our father'; for I tell you, God is able from these stones to raise up children to Abraham. 9Even now the axe is laid to the root of the trees; every tree therefore that does not bear good fruit is cut down and thrown into the fire.
>
> (Lk 3:8–9)

The sentence of destruction pronounced in the parable is just. The people should not think that their escape from the ultimate punishment is owing to their righteousness; it is owing only to the vinedresser's intervention in the hope that they may yet repent. The parable turns a pronouncement of judgment into a call to repentance. A warning is issued: the time is short; God's patience cannot be taken for granted indefinitely. "Even now the axe is laid to the root of the trees." Unless the people repent, God will at the appointed time certainly carry out the sentence of destruction already pronounced.

THE RICH MAN AND LAZARUS

Lk 16:19–31

[19]"There was a rich man, who was clothed in purple
and fine linen and who feasted sumptuously every day.
[20]And at his gate lay a poor man named Lazarus, full of
sores, [21]who desired to be fed with what fell from the rich
man's table; moreover the dogs came and licked his
sores. [22]The poor man died and was carried by the
angels to Abraham's bosom. The rich man also died and
was buried; [23]and in Hades, being in torment, he lifted
up his eyes, and saw Abraham far off and Lazarus in his
bosom. [24]And he called out, 'Father Abraham, have
mercy upon me, and send Lazarus to dip the end of his
finger in water and cool my tongue; for I am in anguish
in this flame.' [25]But Abraham said, 'Son, remember that
you in your lifetime received your good things, and Lazarus in like manner evil things; but now he is comforted
here, and you are in anguish. [26]And besides all this, between us and you a great chasm has been fixed, in order
that those who would pass from here to you may not be
able, and none may cross from there to us.' [27]And he
said, 'Then I beg you, father, to send him to my father's
house, [28]for I have five brothers, so that he may warn
them, lest they also come into this place of torment.'
[29]But Abraham said, 'They have Moses and the prophets;
let them hear them.' [30]And he said, 'No, father Abraham; but if some one goes to them from the dead, they
will repent.' [31]He said to him, 'If they do not hear Moses
and the prophets, neither will they be convinced if some
one should rise from the dead.'"

The exemplary story of the Rich Man and Lazarus is found in Luke's Gospel alone. It is divided into two parts. Part I (vv. 19-26) tells the story of Lazarus and the rich man during this life and the reversal of their fortunes in the next life. This first part is based on an ancient folk tale, known in Egypt and among the Jewish rabbis, about a rich man, a poor man, and the reversal of their lots in the afterlife. Part II of the exemplary story (vv. 27–31) is a dialogue in which a sign is petitioned for and denied.

This is one of the parables based on the contrast between two characters. Its point lies in the reversal of their conditions. The story illustrates the theme struck earlier in Luke: God "has put down the mighty from their thrones, and exalted those of low degree" (Lk 1:52). The emphasis is on the "mighty" one who is put down at the end. The exemplary story is a warning to those who live in this way that unless they repent God's judgment will fall.

Part I of the story (vv. 19–26) begins by portraying the sharply contrasting lives of the two men. The rich man's wealth is shown by his purple and linen garments; these were costly and luxurious. He feasts lavishly, not just on special occasions, but every day. We are to understand not only that he is rich, but also that he is impious, though this is not said explicitly. His unloving attitude toward those in need is indicated by his failure to do anything to relieve Lazarus' poverty and hunger.

Lazarus is a cripple (he lies by the gate, v. 20); his skin sores, evidently not covered by garments at all, are licked by stray dogs. He stays near the gate of the rich man's house to beg from passers-by. The severity of his hunger is shown by his longing for some of the food which falls from the rich man's table (perhaps the reference is to the pieces of bread which guests used to wipe their fingers and then tossed under the table). We are not told explicitly that this beggar is good, only that he is destitute; but his name, Lazarus, which means "God helps," suggests that he is pious. (Only Lazarus is named; the rich man, though often called Dives, is nameless in the story.) In the ancient world, Lazarus would have been regarded as a sinner; his illness and poverty could only be understood as punishment from God. The audience would therefore have been astonished to hear the denouement of the story.

In the afterlife, Lazarus is given the highest place among the righteous. The expression "to Abraham's bosom" means close to Abraham's breast, at his right side at the table (cf. Jn 13:23—people reclined at table); this is the place of honor at the heavenly banquet. Lazarus' condition is completely reversed: on earth he was hungry and despised; in heaven he is seated at the festal table at the highest place of honor.

The rich man's condition, too, is completely reversed. In the afterlife, his fate is the punishment of Hades. His request for a mere drop of water to relieve his torment is a measure of his suffering. Reflected here is the ancient belief that the righteous and the wicked can see each other after death.

The rich man addresses Abraham as his "Father" (v. 24); he expects, as did all descendants of Abraham, to share vicariously in Abraham's merit. Abraham acknowledges the man as his "Son" (v. 25), but the fact that he is Abraham's descendant cannot by itself give him salvation. As we saw in the preaching by John the Baptist (Lk 3:8–9) quoted in the commentary on the Barren Fig Tree, the claim to have Abraham as father—that is, the claim to privileged standing before God—is no substitute for good works.

In Part II of the exemplary story (vv. 27–31), the rich man requests a sign: that Lazarus be sent from the dead to his five living brothers. They must be warned, while there is still time, that the wages for their inhuman life is eternal punishment. Abraham refuses. They have been given Moses and the prophets precisely to convey such teaching. Even a thing as marvelous to see as a resurrection from the dead (v. 31) will not impress those who fail to hear God's word in the Scriptures. (The substance of revelation, fulfilled in Jesus, has been given in Moses and the prophets.)

Jesus is warning those hearers who are in the same position as the rich man's brothers. The brothers stand for the affluent who are indifferent to the poor. Their lives are selfish and unloving. They believe, or live as though they believe, that everything ends with death (v. 28). Such hearers are asking Jesus for a stupendous sign to demonstrate that there is an afterlife and retribution. Jesus denies their request; to grant it would be of no avail. Those who are not converted by the word of God (and Luke includes by implication the Gospel) will not be converted even by the miracle of a resurrection. (In Jn 11:45–53 the raising of Lazarus from the dead only hardens the hearts of the witnesses.) These people may read or hear the Scriptures at worship, but they do not really take hold of their message. The request for a sign is itself an indication of spiritual blindness, deafness, and hardness of heart.

C. The Talents/the Pounds; the Faithful or Unfaithful Servant

The parables considered so far in this chapter were addressed most likely to a general audience. But some of the parables about the eschatological crisis were directed to specific groups, namely, the religious leaders. These were certainly the addressees of the Faithful or Unfaithful Servant, and perhaps also of the Talents or Pounds.

THE TALENTS/THE POUNDS

Mt 25:14–30

[14]"For it will be as when a man going on a journey called his servants and entrusted to them his property; [15]to one he gave five talents, to another

Lk 19:11–27

[11]As they heard these things, he proceeded to tell a parable, because he was near to Jerusalem, and because they supposed that the kingdom of God was to appear immedi-

two, to another one, to each
according to his ability. Then
he went away. [16]He who had
received the five talents went
at once and traded with them;
and he made five talents more.
[17]So also, he who had the two
talents made two talents more.
[18]But he who had received the
one talent went and dug in the
ground and hid his master's
money.

[19]Now after a long time the
master of those servants came
and settled accounts with
them.

[20]And he who had received the
five talents came forward,
bringing five talents more,
saying, 'Master, you delivered
to me five talents; here I have
made five talents more.' [21]His
master said to him,
'Well done, good and faithful
servant; you have been faithful over a little, I will set you
over much; enter into the joy
of your master.'

[22]And he also who had the two
talents came forward saying,
'Master, you delivered to me

ately. [12]He said therefore, "A
nobleman went into a far
country to receive kingly
power and then return. [13]Call-
ing ten of his servants he gave
them ten pounds, and said to
them, 'Trade with these till I
come.'

[14]"But his citizens hated
him and sent an embassy after
him, saying, 'We do not want
this man to reign over us.'
[15]When he returned, having
received the kingly power, he
commanded these servants, to
whom he had given the
money, to be called to him,
that he might know what they
had gained by trading.
[16]The first came before him,

saying, 'Lord, your pound
has made ten pounds more.'
[17]And
he said to him,
'Well done, good
servant! Because you have
been faithful in a very little,
you shall have authority over
ten cities.'

[18]And the second came,
saying, 'Lord, your pound
has made five pounds.'

two talents; here I have made two talents more.' [23]His master said to him, 'Well done, good and faithful servant; you have been faithful over a little, I will set you over much; enter into the joy of your master.' [24]He also who had received the one talent came forward, saying, 'Master, I knew you to be a hard man, reaping where you did not sow, and gathering where you did not winnow; [25]so I was afraid, and I went and hid your talent in the ground. Here you have what is yours.' [26]But his master answered him, 'You wicked and slothful servant! You knew that I reap where I have not sowed, and gather where I have not winnowed? [27]Then you ought to have invested my money with the bankers, and at my coming I should have received what was my own with interest.

[28]So take the talent from him, and give it to him who has the ten talents.

[29]For to every one who has will more be given, and he will have abundance; but from him who has not, even what he has

[19]And he said to him,

'And you are to be over five cities.' [20]Then another came, saying, 'Lord, here is your pound, which I have kept laid away in a napkin; [21]for I was afraid of you, because you are a severe man; you take up what you did not lay down, and reap what you did not sow.' [22]He said to him, 'I will condemn you out of your own mouth, you wicked servant! You knew that I was a severe man, taking up what I did not lay down and reaping what I did not sow? [23]Why then did you not put my money into the bank, and at my coming I should have collected it with interest?' [24]And he said to those who stood by, 'Take the pound from him, and give it to him who has the ten pounds.' [25](And they said to him, 'Lord, he has ten pounds!') [26]'I tell you that to every one who has will more be given;
but from him
who has not, even what he has

will be taken away. [30]And cast the worthless servant into the outer darkness; there men will weep and gnash their teeth.'"

will be taken away. [27]But as for these enemies of mine, who did not want me to reign over them, bring them here and slay them before me.'"

The Talents (Matthew) and the Pounds (Luke) are variants of the same parable. The details of the story in the two Gospels are sufficiently different to suggest that the evangelists did not receive the parable from the same immediate source, Q, but rather from M and L respectively, although we cannot be certain of this. The parable is tentatively assigned to the sources M and L in Appendix II of this book. In any case, the story is substantially the same in the two Gospels, and the two versions no doubt go back to the same original parable.

The differences between the Matthean and Lukan versions are worth noting. Matthew has evidently preserved the parable in an earlier form. Nevertheless, Matthew's version exhibits secondary features. The servants are given talents; since the talent was the largest of all denominations (see the commentary on the Unmerciful Servant), the amounts are enormous, which suggests that for Matthew the "servants" are governors or satraps. Luke's more modest amounts are no doubt original. The Lukan word translated into English as "pound" is *mina* in Greek; a *mina* was equal to 100 denarii, and a denarius was approximately a day's wage (see the commentary on the Laborers in the Vineyard). While in Luke the servants are all given the same amount (one pound each, v. 13), in Matthew they are given different amounts "each according to his ability" (five, two, and one talents respectively, v. 15). This Matthean verse is the origin, incidentally, of the use of the word "talent" to mean native ability, which differs from person to person. In Matthew, the unprofitable servant is at least careful and responsible: he buries the money in the earth (vv. 18, 25). In Luke, however, he is utterly careless and irresponsible: he hides the money in a napkin (v. 20). According to rabbinic law, burying is the best safeguard against theft (see the commentary on the Treasure), and one who buries entrusted money is free from liability; but anyone who wraps entrusted money in cloth is obliged to restore any loss incurred through such incaution. Finally, the rewards and punishments are this-worldly and more realistic in Luke (vv. 17, 19, 24). In Matthew, an other-worldly reward and punishment are added (vv. 21, 23, 30).

In Luke we find a complex of variations which calls for separate comment. Matthew's "man" (v. 14) or "master" (v. 19), probably a merchant, becomes in Luke a "nobleman" who goes on a journey to claim a kingdom (v. 12; the English translation reads "kingly power" in vv. 12 and 15, but the original Greek is "kingdom"). His fellow citizens attempt to obstruct his plan by dispatching emissaries to protest his installation as their ruler, but he succeeds despite them in receiving the kingdom (vv. 14–15), and returns to have his enemies slain in his sight (v. 27). What we have in Luke is one of the few instances in the Gospels of the conflation, or combination, of two parables (another occurs in Matthew's Great Feast and Wedding Garment). Luke, or more likely a predecessor of his, has introduced into the story of the Pounds a separate story about a nobleman, disliked by his countrymen, seeking a kingdom; that story appears in vv. 12, 14, 15, and 27, and in the authority over ten cities and five cities given to the first two servants in vv. 17 and 19. The story is reminiscent of a historical incident. In 4 B.C., Herod the Great's son, Archelaus, journeyed to Rome for confirmation of his kingship over Judea (the southern part of Palestine); the Jews sent an embassy of 50 persons to Rome to protest his appointment. Archelaus received the confirmation from Rome and returned to Judea to wreak bloody revenge on the people. Possibly Jesus (or the primitive Church) drew on this event to create a parable about the crisis of the end-times which is lost except for these fragments in Luke's parable of the Pounds. The parable warns the hearers against a false sense of security: destruction may fall unexpectedly, as unexpectedly as Archelaus' revenge. Once these intrusions are removed,

Luke's parable of the Pounds is much the same as Matthew's parable of the Talents.

Excluding the Lukan story of the nobleman, and removing the secondary features in the Matthean and Lukan versions of the remaining story of the Talents or Pounds, we arrive at the following main lines of the parable. A merchant calls three of his servants; the number three appears often in folk tales. He gives each one a sum of money in trust, and goes on a journey. He gives the trust either to avoid leaving his capital unused during his absence, or to test his servants' faithfulness. Upon his return, he calls his servants in to render account. The first two servants have invested the money and increased their master's capital; they are commended and rewarded with an even greater trust. The third servant admits that, too timid and fearful to invest the money, he has hoarded it, and earned no profit for his master; he returns to the master the exact sum he had been given in trust. If he expects to receive praise for his caution and honesty, he is disappointed. The master severely reprimands him: "You wicked and slothful servant! You knew that I reap where I have not sowed, and gather where I have not winnowed? Then you ought to have invested my money with the bankers, and at my coming I should have received what was my own with interest" (Mt 25:26–27; cf. Lk 19:22–23). It is in these words of the master that Matthew and Luke are in closest agreement. The unenterprising servant's trust is taken from him and given to the most enterprising servant. The original story probably ended here.

In the original parable, the emphasis lies on the reckoning and on the unprofitable servant. The master's departure serves only as an occasion for the servants' testing; it has no other significance. The hearers are invited to pass judgment on all the servants, but particularly on the unenterprising one. Not only is he too cowardly to take the means to make profitable use of what is entrusted to him; the money which he has left in disuse is not his own, but someone else's. He has been unfaithful in his trust. For this he is called "wicked" (Mt 25:26; Lk 19:22).

The lesson of the parable is clear. The first two servants are rewarded for their faithfulness, courage, and activity; the third servant is punished for his unfaithfulness, cowardice and inactivity. The excuse advanced by the unprofitable servant, that the master is demanding, should instead have been the motive for him to act. It is a spiritual law—as it is a law in so many areas of life (physical and intellectual activity, financial investment)—that neglect and disuse of our gifts result in loss. According to Matthew, the unprofitable servant of God is punished with eternal damnation.

For Jesus' audience, whom did the servants, and especially the unfaithful one, represent? In the Old Testament and in Judaism down to Jesus' time, the figure of servants was a standard metaphor for the Israelite people, and the figure of the lord or master a standard metaphor for God. The third servant, then, stands for a certain group among the people—but there is no indication as to who specifically this is. Some exegetes say the servants stand for God's people in general; much has been entrusted to them, and they will soon have to render an account as to what use they have made of their special trust. Other interpreters believe the unprofitable servant stands for the Pharisees, whose emphasis on tradition and the law and whose exclusion of certain groups (unfortunately attitudes still among us in some quarters today), made their religion sterile, that is, of no benefit to others. Yet other commentators think that Jesus had in mind the religious leaders; God's revelation had been entrusted to them, but they may have stifled and rendered it inoperative. Whoever the audience to whom the parable was originally addressed, it is not difficult to see its relevance for today. In any case, the command, "Take the pound from him, and give it to him who has the ten pounds" (Lk 19:24; cf. Mt 25:28), means that God will now give the trust to others. In the original parable, as noted, this was the punishment of the unfaithful servant and the conclusion of the story.

The early Church and the evangelists expanded the parable in two ways in order to apply it to its own situation. First (before the parable reached Matthew and Luke), this saying was added: "I tell you that to every one who has will more be given; but from him who has not, even what he has will be taken away" (Lk 19:26; cf. Mt 25:29). This proverb was originally an isolated saying of Jesus; it appears in a very different context in Mk 4:25. Its addition to the parable has the effect of giving primary emphasis to a secondary point in the parable: the manner of divine retribution. It seems unjust (Lk 19:25), but, the proverb says, this is what God's justice is like.

Secondly, the Church and the evangelists expanded and reapplied the parable by introducing the theme of the parousia. The journey of the master is now given great significance: the master stands for Jesus; his departure for Jesus' death, resurrection, and ascension; and his return for the parousia and judgment. In Luke, this theme appears in the introduction, in which Jesus cautions that the consummation of God's reign is not imminent (Lk 19:11). According to Luke's introduction, the parable is told to correct the false expectations of God's reign immediately, and to teach that the interval before its coming will be a time of testing. In Matthew, the theme of the parousia appears in two places: the saying "enter into the joy of your master" (25:21, 23, missing in Luke), which probably refers to the feast of salvation, and the command that the servant be cast "into the outer darkness" (25:30, missing in Luke), which refers to eternal punishment. Both are related to the parousia.

THE FAITHFUL OR UNFAITHFUL SERVANT

Mt 24:45–51	Lk 12:42–46
	42 And the Lord said,
45 "Who then is the faithful and wise servant, whom his master has set over his household, to give them their	"Who then is the faithful and wise steward, whom his master will set over his household, to give them their

food at the proper time?

[46]Blessed is that servant whom his master when he comes will find so doing. [47]Truly I say to you, he will set him over all his possessions. [48]But if that wicked servant says to himself, 'My master is delayed,' [49]and begins to beat his fellow servants, and
eats and drinks with the drunken, [50]the master of that servant will come on a day when he does not expect him and at an hour he does not know, [51]and will punish him, and put him with the hypocrites; there men will weep and gnash their teeth."

portion of food at the proper time?
[43]Blessed is that servant whom his master when he comes will find so doing. [44]Truly I tell you, he will set him over all his possessions. [45]But if that servant says to himself, 'My master is delayed in coming,' and begins to beat the menservants and the maidservants, and to eat and drink and get drunk, [46]the master of that servant will come on a day when he does not expect him and at an hour he does not know, and will punish him, and put him with the unfaithful."

This parable, preserved in Q, was incorporated faithfully by both Matthew and Luke. There are only a few minor differences in the versions we find in the two Gospels. The parable is introduced with a question, which reflects the nature of a parable as intended to provoke the hearer to thought and decision.

This is one of those parables the meaning of which is based on contrast. Some commentators believe the contrast is between two servants who conduct themselves differently; but more likely there is only one servant in the parable, who may behave in either of two ways. The servant is placed in a position of responsibility during the period of his master's absence. The question is whether during this time he will be faithful to his trust or will betray it. The faithful servant is one who treats his fellow servants with justice. He will be rewarded with greater responsibility. The unfaithful servant is one who oppresses his fellow servants and indulges himself. Such a servant, forgetting his servanthood, comes to imagine that *he* is the master. The master's unexpected return will reveal how the servant has behaved toward the other servants.

Matthew speaks of the servant's "*fellow* servants" (v. 49); this shows him to be only a servant among servants. Luke speaks of "menservants and *maid*servants" (v. 45); today Luke would say that women and men have an equal claim to be treated justly.

We must inquire first as to the original meaning of the parable when uttered by Jesus. What would the figure of the servant placed in authority and tested by his master's unexpected return mean to Jesus' audience?

This parable is directed to religious leaders. The fact that the servant is placed in authority makes this clear. In the Old Testament, rulers, prophets, and sacred persons are called "servants of God" (e.g., Moses in Num 12:7; the prophets in 2 Kgs 17:13). Jesus' hearers, familiar with this Old Testament designation, would have thought of the religious leaders of their own time—the priests and scribes (see Mt 23:13; Lk 11:52). This parable suggests that the religious rulers have been unfaithful servants (as does the Wicked Tenants and perhaps also the Talents or Pounds). The parable was a warning to the religious leaders that the day of testing was at hand when God would reveal whether or not they had abused the authority entrusted to them.

As it appears in the Gospels of Matthew and Luke, the parable is applied to the early Church's situation: it is now addressed to Church leaders. As the context shows, the master is interpreted as the Son of man (Mt 24:44; Lk 12:40); the master's journey is understood as the time between the death and resurrection of Jesus and the parousia; the master's return is interpreted as the final judgment; and the punishment is now eternal (Mt 24:51; Lk 12:46). The parable warns Church leaders not to allow the delay of the parousia to be an excuse for unfaithfulness. Evidently some Church leaders were unfaithful to their commitment as servants.

This parable could be entitled "Authoritarianism and Servanthood." What is significant about the parable is that the religious leaders' unfaithfulness consists in their abuse of authority. The religious leader is a servant among servants. Religious leaders are not excused from the obligation to treat their fellow maidservants and menservants with justice in every way.

D. *The Wicked Tenants*

In the parable of the Wicked Tenants, Jesus issues his final warning to the religious leaders. In it, he tells how God has made his final and definitive appeal through him, how it is rejected, and how despite this and even because of it God's reign will be opened to all believers.

THE WICKED TENANTS

Mt 21:33–43	Mk 12:1–11	Lk 20:9–18
[33]Hear another parable. There was a householder who planted a vineyard,	[1]And he began to speak to them in parables. "A man planted a vineyard,	[9]And he began to tell the people this parable: "A man planted a vineyard,
and set a hedge around it, and dug a wine press in it, and built a tower,	and set a hedge around it, and dug a pit for the wine press, and built a tower,	
and let it out to tenants, and went into another country.	and let it out to tenants, and went into another country.	and let it out to tenants, and went into another country for a long while.
[34]When the season of fruit drew near, he sent his servants	[2]When the time came, he sent a servant	[10]When the time came, he sent a servant

to the tenants to get his fruit;	to the tenants, to get from them some of the fruit of the vineyard.	to the tenants, that they should give him some of the fruit of the vineyard;
35 and the tenants took his servants and beat one, killed another, and stoned another.	3 And they took him and beat him, and sent him away empty-handed.	but the tenants beat him, and sent him away empty-handed.
36 Again, he sent other servants, more than the first; and they did the same to them.	4 Again he sent to them another servant, and they wounded him in the head, and treated him shamefully.	11 And he sent another servant; him also they beat and treated shamefully, and sent him away empty-handed.
	5 And he sent another, and him they killed; and so with many others, some they beat and some they killed.	12 And he sent yet a third; this one they wounded and cast out.
37 Afterward he sent his son to them, saying, 'They will respect my son.'	6 He had still one other, a beloved son; finally he sent him to them, saying, 'They will respect my son.'	13 Then the owner of the vineyard said, 'What shall I do? I will send my beloved son; it may be they will respect him.'
38 But when the tenants saw the son, they said to themselves, 'This is the heir; come, let us kill him and have his inheritance.'	7 But those tenants said to one another, 'This is the heir; come, let us kill him, and the inheritance will be ours.'	14 But when the tenants saw him, they said to themselves, 'This is the heir; let us kill him, that the inheritance may be ours.'
39 And they took him and cast him out of	8 And they took him and killed him, and	15 And they cast him

the vineyard, and killed him. 40 When therefore the owner of the vineyard comes, what will he do to those tenants?" 41 They said to him,	cast him out of the vineyard. 9 What will the owner of the vineyard do?	out of the vineyard and killed him. What then will the owner of the vineyard do to them?
"He will put those wretches to a miserable death, and let out the vineyard to other tenants who will give him the fruits in their seasons."	He will come and destroy the tenants and give the vineyard to others.	16 He will come and destroy those tenants, and give the vineyard to others."
		When they heard this, they said, "God forbid!"
42 Jesus said to them, "Have you never read in the scriptures:	10 Have you not read this scripture:	17 But he looked at them and said, "What then is this that is written:
'The very stone which the builders rejected has become the head of the corner; this was the Lord's doing, and it is marvelous in our eyes'?	'The very stone which the builders rejected has become the head of the corner; 11 this was the Lord's doing, and it is marvelous in our eyes'?"	'The very stone which the builders rejected has become the head of the corner'?
43 Therefore I tell you, the kingdom of God will be taken away from you and given to a nation producing the fruits of it."		18 Every one who falls on that stone will be broken to pieces; but when it falls on any one it will crush him."

The parable of the Wicked Tenants appears in all three Synoptic Gospels; it was taken by Matthew and Luke from Mark. The authenticity of this parable was long doubted, because it seems unrealistic, because it has references to historical figures and events, and because it ends with a prediction of the death of Jesus, which some think could not have come from Jesus himself. In recent decades, however, a number of commentators have argued for its authenticity. Jesus probably addressed this parable to the religious leaders, the priests, scribes, and elders, as the Gospels report (Mk 11:27; 12:12; Mt 21:23, 45; Lk 20:1, 19).

The parable is set against the socio-economic and political background of first-century Palestine, especially the northern region, Galilee (Jesus' home district). The climate was one of unrest and revolution. Many large estates were owned by absentee landlords, often foreigners. The economic discontent of tenant farmers was joined to a strong nationalist sentiment. The withholding of rent, violence, and the seizure of land by peasants were not unknown. To collect the produce of his land, due him as rent, the landlord would send his agents. The law provided for the right of anyone to claim unowned property. Evidently on some such legal grounds, the tenants in this parable assume that the death of the sole heir, the landlord's son, will give them legal right to claim the property (v. 7). The parable is thus more realistic than might at first appear.

Exegetes have suggested that the following outline may represent the original version of the parable. An absentee landlord lets out his vineyard to tenant cultivators. It is agreed that the tenants will pay rent in the form of a portion of the produce. At vintage time, the landlord sends two agents, one at a time, to collect the rent. They are affronted, beaten, and driven out. The landlord, concerned about the seriousness of the situation, sends his son to deal with it, assuming that he will command respect. The tenants, however, murder the son, cast his body out of the vineyard, leaving it unburied—the ultimate indignity—and seize the property.

In Mark's Gospel (and in Matthew's), the opening of the parable, narrating the careful construction of the vineyard, is a clear reference to the Song of the Vineyard in Is 5:1–7. This detailed beginning, missing in Luke's Gospel, may be secondary. Isaiah's Song of the Vineyard begins:

> Let me sing for my beloved a love song concerning his vineyard; My beloved had a vineyard on a very fertile hill. [2]He digged it and cleared it of stones, and planted it with choice vines; he built a watchtower in the midst of it, and hewed out a wine vat in it;
>
> Is 5:1–2

The Isaian passage, even if only hinted at as in Luke's version, would have been familiar to Jesus' Jewish audience. From this allusion, they would have known that the vineyard stands for Israel and the owner for God: "For the vineyard of the Lord of hosts is the house of Israel" (Is 5:7). These were standard metaphors in the Old Testament and Judaism, beginning with Isaiah's Song of the Vineyard. It follows that the tenants in the parable stand for the religious leaders of Israel. According to the Gospels, the priests, scribes, and elders "perceived that he had told the parable against them" (Mk 12:12; cf. Mt 21:45; Lk 20:19); there is no reason to doubt the historicity of this verse. These metaphors, then, are most likely original constituent meanings of the parable.

In the parable as we find it in the Gospels, the servants or agents stand for the prophets of Israel. It is not certain whether Jesus himself intended this reference or whether it is secondary. The original parable, as suggested above, may have had only two servants and one son; the number three is common in folk stories. The expansion of the number of servants, and the series of insults and injuries (in the three Gospels), culminating in murder (in Mark and Matthew), may be secondary features; they are certainly intended to allude to the long line of Israelite prophets, who were rejected and persecuted.

The son in the parable stands for Jesus. Some doubt that Jesus himself intended this figure to point to him, since he would then be predicting his own death; but it is difficult not to see in the son an original reference to Jesus. For one thing, in the Markan version there is no reflection of the manner of Jesus' death, which suggests that the parable was composed before that event. For another, the story ends abruptly with the son's murder; the resurrection, of central importance for the early Church, is not mentioned in the parable itself, so that it is unlikely that we have in the metaphor of the son a creation by the early Church. Jesus evidently did regard his ministry as the climax of God's dealings with the people. No doubt in the figure of the son he intended a reference to his own mission. Many interpreters now believe that Jesus may well have anticipated his approaching death at the hands of his enemies.

The christological allusion was later heightened by the early Church, however, by the following means: the use of the adjective "beloved" of the son (Mk 12:6; cf. Mk 1:11; 9:7), and, as we shall see, the change in the order of events surrounding the son's death to suggest the crucifixion (Mt 21:39; Lk 20:15), and the addition of the metaphor of the rejected stone made into the cornerstone (Mk 12:10–11), which provides the missing reference to the resurrection.

The parable ends with a question eliciting a judgment: "What will the owner of the vineyard do?" (Mk 12:9a). The question refers to Is 5:5: "And now I will tell you what I will do to my vineyard." According to Mark, Jesus answers the parable's concluding question himself; ordinarily he does not, and this feature may be inauthentic. (Matthew reverts to the usual form, and has the audience respond in 21:41.) The reply states that the landlord will crush the tenants' rebellion and let out the vineyard to others (Mk 12:9b). We have here a reference to the disruption of the religious leadership. In Mark and Luke, the "others" to whose care the vineyard is given over no doubt stand for "the poor," the marginalized and despised. It is uncertain whether the question and answer are original or secondary.

The more important redactional changes which Matthew made in his Markan source are worth noting. The servants are sent out in two missions (vv. 34–36); they are intended to stand for the pre-exilic and post-exilic prophets, or the "former" and "latter" prophets of the Hebrew Bible. In Matthew (and in Luke), the order of events around the son's death is changed. He is first cast out of the vineyard and then killed (Mt 21:39; Lk 20:15); the allusion is to the crucifixion of Jesus outside the city of Jerusalem (see Jn 19:17; Heb 13:12-13). The expression "put those wretches to a miserable death" (v. 41) is a reference to the capture of Jerusalem by the Romans in A.D. 70. The "other tenants who will give him the fruits in their seasons" (v. 41) and "a nation producing the fruits of it" (v. 43) suggest the Gentile Church. Thus in Matthew the "others" are no longer the poor, as in Mark and Luke, but the Gentiles. We have here an allusion to the rejection of Israel and the election of the Gentiles. V. 43 makes this a parable of the kingdom of God. Matthew has transformed the parable into a schematic outline of salvation history (as he did the parable of the Great Feast), spanning Israel, Jesus, and the Church.

Appended to the parable in all three Gospels is a citation of Ps 118:22–23 (Mk 12:10–11; Mt 21:42; Lk 20–17). This is not an original part of the parable. The mataphor of the rejected stone become the cornerstone adds an otherwise lacking reference to the resurrection. Ps 118:22–23 was a favorite text in the early Church for the resurrection and exaltation of Jesus Christ (see Acts 4:11; 1 Pt 2:7). Luke has added (v. 18) still another text from Is 8:14–15 about a stone which destroys those who fall on it and those on whom it falls (cf. 1 Pt 2:8). The Old Testament quotations heighten the christological significance of the parable; the early Church evidently attached importance to this parable and spelled out its meaning in an unmistakable way.

Appendix I

THE PARABLES IN EACH SYNOPTIC GOSPEL

MARK

Parable	**The Sower**	4:3-9,14-20
Similitude	**The Growing Seed**	4:26-29
Similitude	**The Mustard Seed**	4:30-32
Parable	**The Wicked Tenants**	12:1-11

MATTHEW

Similitude	**The Two Builders**	7:24-27
Parable	**The Sower**	13:3-9,18-23
Parable	**The Weeds and the Wheat**	13:24-30,36-43
Similitude	**The Mustard Seed**	13:31-32
Similitude	**The Leaven**	13:33
Parable	**The Treasure**	13:44
Parable	**The Pearl**	13:45-46
Similitude	**The Fishnet**	13:47-50
Similitude	**The Lost Sheep**	18:12-14
Parable	**The Unmerciful Servant**	18:23-35
Parable	**The Laborers in the Vineyard**	20:1-16
Parable	**The Two Sons**	21:28-32
Parable	**The Wicked Tenants**	21:33-43
Parable	**The Great Feast; The Wedding Garment**	22:2-10,11-14
Similitude	**The Faithful or Unfaithful Servant**	24:45-51
Parable	**The Ten Maidens**	25:1-13
Parable	**The Talents (The Pounds)**	25:14-30

LUKE

Similitude	**The Two Builders**	6:47-49
Parable	**The Two Debtors**	7:41-43
Parable	**The Sower**	8:5-8,11-15
Exemplary Story	**The Good Samaritan**	10:29-37
Similitude	**The Friend at Midnight**	11:5-8
Exemplary Story	**The Rich Fool**	12:16-21
Similitude	**The Faithful or Unfaithful Servant**	12:42-46
Parable	**The Barren Fig Tree**	13:6-9
Similitude	**The Mustard Seed**	13:18-19
Similitude	**The Leaven**	13:20-21
Parable	**The Great Feast**	14:15-24
Similitude	**The Tower Builder**	14:28-30
Similitude	**The Warring King**	14:31-32
Similitude	**The Lost Sheep**	15:3-7
Similitude	**The Lost Coin**	15:8-10
Parable	**The Prodigal Son**	15:11-32
Parable	**The Unjust Steward**	16:1-8
Exemplary Story	**The Rich Man and Lazarus**	16:19-31
Similitude	**The Master and Servant**	17:7-10
Parable	**The Persistent Widow**	18:1-8
Exemplary Story	**The Pharisee and the Tax Collector**	18:9-14
Parable	**The Pounds (The Talents)**	19:11-27
Parable	**The Wicked Tenants**	20:9-18

Note: It is difficult in a few cases to decide whether an utterance of Jesus is to be included among the parables (in the broad sense). It is also difficult to decide whether some parables are *similitudes* or *parables* (in the narrow sense). While there is a large area of agreement among New Testament interpreters on these points, there is also some diversity of opinion.

Appendix II

THE SOURCES OF THE PARABLES

Matthew and Luke worked independently of each other, but each employed two sources, Mark and Q (a collection of Jesus' teaching), in the composition of his Gospel. In addition, each had special material which we designate M and L respectively. Thus Matthew drew his parables from Mark, Q and M, Luke from Mark, Q and L. The sources for the Synoptic parables are these four, Mark, Q, M and L. The parables are here listed according to their sources.

MARK

		Mark	Matthew	Luke
Parable	**The Sower**	4:3-9, 14-20	13:3-9, 18-23	8:5-8, 11-15
Similitude	**The Growing Seed**	4:26-29		
Similitude	**The Mustard Seed (also in Q)**	4:30-32	13:31-32	13:18-19
Parable	**The Wicked Tenants**	12:1-11	21:33-43	20:9-18

Q

		Mark	Matthew	Luke
Similitude	**The Two Builders**		7:24-27	6:47-49
Similitude	**The Mustard Seed (also in Mk)**	4:30-32	13:31-32	13:18-19
Similitude	**The Leaven**		13:33	13:20-21
Similitude	**The Lost Sheep**		18:12-14	15:3-7
Parable	**The Great Feast**		22:2-10	14:15-24
Similitude	**The Faithful or Unfaithful Servant**		24:45-51	12:42-46

Parable	**The Talents / The Pounds**		25:14-30	19:11-27

M

		Mark	Matthew	Luke
Parable	**The Weeds and the Wheat**		13:24-30, 36-43	
Parable	**The Treasure**		13:44	
Parable	**The Pearl**		13:45-46	
Similitude	**The Fishnet**		13:47-50	
Parable	**The Unmerciful Servant**		18:23-35	
Parable	**The Laborers in the Vineyard**		20:1-16	
Parable	**The Two Sons**		21:28-32	
Parable	**The Wedding Garment**		22:11-14	
Parable	**The Ten Maidens**		25:1-13	

L

		Mark	Matthew	Luke
Parable	**The Two Debtors**			7:41-43
Exemplary Story	**The Good Samaritan**			10:29-37
Similitude	**The Friend at Midnight**			11:5-8
Exemplary Story	**The Rich Fool**			12:16-21
Parable	**The Barren Fig Tree**			13:6-9
Similitude	**The Tower Builder**			14:28-30
Similitude	**The Warring King**			14:31-32
Similitude	**The Lost Coin**			15:8-10
Parable	**The Prodigal Son**			15:11-32
Parable	**The Unjust Steward**			16:1-8
Exemplary Story	**The Rich Man and Lazarus**			16:19-31

Similitude	**The Master and Servant**	17:7-10
Parable	**The Persistent Widow**	18:1-8
Exemplary Story	**The Pharisee and the Tax Collector**	18:9-14

FOR FURTHER READING

1. FOR THE GENERAL READER

The following are excellent introductions to the parables:

Wilfrid J. Harrington. *A Key to the Parables.* Glen Rock, N.J.: Paulist Press, 1964.

__________, *Parables Told by Jesus: A Contemporary Approach to the Parables.* New York: Alba House, 1971.

Archibald M. Hunter. *Interpreting the Parables.* Philadelphia, Pa.: Westminster, 1960.

__________, *The Parables Then and Now.* Philadelphia, Pa.: Westminster, 1971.

Jan Lambrecht. *Parables of Jesus: Insight and Challenge.* Trans. René Van de Walle and Christopher Begg. Bangalore, India: Theological Publications in India, 1978.

Eta Linnemann. American title: *Jesus of the Parables: Introduction and Exposition.* Trans. John Sturdy. New York: Harper & Row, 1967. British title: *Parables of Jesus: Introduction and Exposition.* Trans. John Sturdy. London: SPCK, 1966.

Jacques Dupont. *Pourquoi des paraboles? La méthode parabolique de Jésus.* Lire la Bible 46. Paris: Editions du Cerf, 1977.

For the reader of French, an interesting, brief treatment of the subject of the parables, the audience and mode of communication, and the way in which the parables achieve their effect.

2. FOR THE MORE ADVANCED STUDENT

Madeleine Boucher. *The Mysterious Parable: A Literary Study.* Washington, D.C.: Catholic Biblical Association of America, 1977.

Analysis of the parable as a literary construct, with special attention to the problem of parable and allegory, and to the place of the parable in the Markan theme of mystery.

C. H. Dodd. *The Parables of the Kingdom.* rev. ed. New York: Scribner's, 1961.
Shows the relation of the parables to Jesus' preaching of the reign of God, and argues that we must attempt to discover the original meaning of the parables in Jesus' ministry.

Joachim Jeremias. *The Parables of Jesus.* rev. ed. Trans. S. H. Hooke. New York: Scribner's, 1963.
More detailed study along the course charted by Dodd.

__________, *Rediscovering the Parables.* Trans. S. H. Hooke and Frank Clarke. New York: Scribner's, 1966.
Abridged and less technical version of the preceding book.

3. BIBLIOGRAPHIES

The following provide extensive bibliographies for the parables in general as well as for individual parables:

Warren S. Kissinger. *The Parables of Jesus: A History of Interpretation and Bibliography.* Metuchen, N.J./London: Scarecrow Press and American Theological Library Association, 1979. Pp. 231-415.

Semeia 1 (an experimental journal for biblical criticism), 1974. Pp. 236-74.

4. HELPFUL TOOL

Burton H. Throckmorton, Jr., ed. *Gospel Parallels: A Synopsis of the First Three Gospels.* 4th ed. Toronto/Camden, N.J./London: Thomas Nelson, 1979.
Synoptic Gospels printed in parallel columns for comparison.